THE TEEN KILLER WHISPERER

How I Discovered the Causes, Warning Signs
and Triggers of Teen Killers and School Shooters

PHIL CHALMERS

Lulu Publishing Services rev. date: 12/26/2019

CONTENTS

MY STORY
INTRODUCTION

Born and raised on the gritty streets of Cleveland, Ohio, growing up I experienced poverty, crime, dysfunction, alcoholism, and instability. I was robbed on my way to school, experienced intruders breaking into our home at night, and had to be constantly aware of my surroundings in the fast-changing and unsafe city of Cleveland, Ohio.

*The site of my former rat-infested apartment
that I lived in the first ten years of my life.*

Although my home wasn't reminiscent of "Leave it to Beaver," and although I experienced poverty and dysfunction, I do remember some good times, playing with my younger brother, visits to amusement parks, camping trips, playing with our pedal car, watching stock car racing, Christmas trees and presents, and Santa Claus.

*With my younger brother in our gravel yard
playing with a homemade pedal car.*

*My brother and I with my father, who rarely
was pictured without a beer and cigarette.*

Around the time I was ten years old and had just completed the fifth grade at a catholic school in Cleveland, my family finally escaped the dangerous city and moved to a suburb of Cleveland, which was a culture shock for all of us. We now lived in a safe, small town with large homes and residents that included local celebrities like newscasters and professional football players. My parents inherited a building lot from my grandfather and built a house themselves, which is the only way they could afford living in this upscale town. It took me a few years to fully acclimate to the suburban lifestyle, but I eventually did, playing on school sports teams and making friends in our little all-American town.

*I diverted my anger and violence towards
sports in middle school and high school.*

I enjoyed playing sports in high school, playing football and wrestling, and I took out a lot of my anger and frustration in the weight room. My role model and father figure in high school was my football coach, who was good to me. With my coach believing in me, for the first time, I realized I could be somebody, and I could accomplish my goals and dreams.

In our family, I felt like I was my mother's favorite, and my brother was by father's favorite. I received good grades in school, rarely got into trouble, and fed my entrepreneurial spirit, starting my own lawn mowing business, selling golf balls at our local country club, and launching my speaking company, mostly targeting troubled kids.

My younger brother, my lone sibling, loved to hunt and fish, which are my father's favorite hobbies. My brother also liked to work with his hands, like my father, so there was a natural connection between the two. I had a connection with my mother, mainly because her interests were more like mine. When my brother took over the family business, he solidified his position in the family as "the favorite son".

Because I was more interested in working in the occupation of helping and saving kids, public speaking and writing, I further drove a wedge between myself and my father when I didn't follow in the family business, repairing greasy electric motors. I would use my upbringing and dysfunction as fuel to drive me to success, but I seemed to be always trying to earn my parents approval, especially my father.

Over the next two decades, I stayed connected to my family, but I kept my distance, mostly seeing them on holidays. I have learned in life that everyone has a story, and people react and do things based on the way they were raised, and the way they were treated. So instead of holding grudges and spreading hate, I have learned to forgive and move on, instead doing my best to spread peace, love and forgiveness. And in my experience, it has served me well.

The main reason I am healthy and successful today is because I am a spiritual person, I have faith in God, and I have learned about forgiveness. And although I am quick to forgive those who have wronged me, I never forget. I also try not to place myself into a relationship that is unhealthy, be it a spouse, a friend, or acquaintances.

The reason for talking about my upbringing is many people ask me why I do what I do. One of the reasons is I can relate to those who commit these violent crimes-I understand them. The killers and I have a connection, because many times we were raised in the same types of neighborhoods with the same types of families, with the same types of circumstances. It creates a connection, and allows me to gather the information from them that so many are seeking.

After high school I attended two years of college. At first, I thought I wanted to major in business and become an accountant. I quickly realized this was not my destiny or my passion. I had a desire to help children and young adults, and felt a connection to those who had a similar upbringing as mine. I wanted to help save the kids who grew up in homes like mine, to show them that no matter what their circumstances were, they could succeed in life like I did.

I began working with violent offenders through a church program in Cleveland, many of them rapists and killers. It was through this program that I got my first taste of working with young felons dressed in prison orange uniforms in a maximum-security juvenile prison. I was only eighteen years old, but I was hooked. I could relate to their pain, anger and dysfunction, because I could have easily been sitting there in lock up just like them. And they knew it. I realized I could make my pain my passion, and use my story to help others. And the rest, as they say, is history.

I also began speaking to other youth around Ohio, and soon thereafter, all throughout the United States. I realized that I had a gift of speaking to others that I wanted to use. I spoke to young people about destructive decisions, and challenged them to make better choices. I had a passion to steer teens from bullying, alcohol and drug addiction, as well as violent entertainment. I felt if they could make better choices in their lives, they could live a life that God intended, which includes a life of peace, love and stability.

After a few years of doing this, I began noticing that teens were committing murders nationwide. So I began to communicate with these teen killers and school shooters, something that I still do today. In 1990, I conducted my first death row interview, interviewing a satanic teen killer named Sean Sellers on Oklahoma's death row. He was one of the youngest teens sentenced to death in the country, for three murders, and he was eventually one of the youngest teens put to death. After that interview, my future was crystal clear, and I knew what my contribution to the world would be, to interview as many killers as I could, discover what factors contributed to the violent acts they committed, and share what I learned with the world. Thirty years later, that is exactly what I have done.

*My first face-to-face death row interview
with Satanic teen killer, Sean Sellers.*

After the Sean Sellers interview, I continued to speak to teens across the country at camps, conferences, schools and retreats. I occasionally interviewed a killer who I had an interest in, with early interviews including serial killer David "Son of Sam" Berkowitz, school shooter Evan Ramsey from Alaska, and Amityville Horror's Ronald Defeo. But everything changed for me on April 20, 1999, while I was living in Ohio. I watched in horror as two students took over a school in Colorado, shooting and killing thirteen people. I also observed how the news media and the so-called "experts" struggled to explain why this happened. Quite frankly, they seemed to have no idea. I wasn't sure either, but on April 21, 1999, I began my research project to interview as many teen killers and school shooters that I could, face-to-face, and discover once and for all why they were killing their families, their girlfriends, and their innocent classmates. And discover I did.

I saw a distinct pattern of the causes, warning signs and triggers of juvenile homicide. Therefore, for ten years, I documented my research and interviews, and wrote my first major book. On the ten-year anniversary of the Columbine Massacre, on April 20, 2009, I released the book "Inside the Mind of a Teen Killer," which has been my most successful project to date, selling thousands and thousands of copies. Released by a major publisher and sitting on book shelves in all of the major book stores, it was a very proud accomplishment for me. With the release of this new book, I began training and speaking to adults instead of teens, which was new ground for me.

My first book release with a major publisher,
hitting bookstores nationwide.

INSIDE THE MIND OF A TEEN KILLER

With the release of "Inside the Mind of a Teen Killer" I began a new career as a police trainer, teen violence expert, and television personality. Over the last ten years I have trained law enforcement of all levels, homicide teams, the FBI, Homeland Security, coroners, school administrators, juvenile justice members, probation officers, counselors, clergy, officers of the court and just about anyone who had an interest in helping youth and preventing violence among this population. I have trained in each of our great fifty states, and I continue to crisscross the country multiple times a year. Hotel rooms, airports, rental cars, resort towns and suitcases have became my way of life.

A new avenue for the dissemination of my research was presented to me, working with television production companies and major news media outlets to share my knowledge on television. It has been one of the most exciting opportunities thus far in my career, allowing me to share my knowledge with the masses. I have appeared on dozens of networks, filmed in places from Beverly Hills to seedy prisons, with my most recognized work being A&E's Killer Kids and Fox's Crime Watch Daily.

My work was also featured in a major new magazine, which taught me a lesson about trusting the media. The article was biased and negative in nature, with the only positive being the title, "The Teen Killer Whisperer." I learned very quickly through this experience that the mainstream media wasn't searching for the truth, but only their version of the truth. I could no longer trust them to get this ever-important information out-I had to do it myself, and that is exactly what I have done for the past decade, conducting 150-180 day-long trainings annually around the country.

I spend a lot of my time training police officers and homicide detectives.

MY ADULT LIFE

My adult life hasn't been all rainbows and butterflies, as I have gone through some challenging times just like everyone else. At the age of twenty three, I made the mistake of getting married too young and to the wrong person. Because I didn't want to disappoint my family or be a statistic of divorce, knowing how much it hurts children, I stayed married to my first wife for 25 years. The last ten years were not good, and the same dysfunction I experienced growing up now became a reality in my own home. The marriage grew to become super unhealthy, so I knew it was time to pull the trigger, and divorce this woman. My only hope was that God would lead me a healthy and stable wife, who would support my life's work of helping others.

Disappointed that I had wasted decades of my life with the wrong spouse, God led me to my soulmate and my current wife, who has been a godsend. Her name is as unique as she is, Wendi spelled with an "i." She is as beautiful on the inside as she is on the outside, and believe me, she is very beautiful on the outside. She was the principal at a school I spoke at in 2013, when we met. So as the story goes, the guest speaker met the principal, and the rest is history. Was it easy? Absolutely not. Was it worth it? You better believe it.

On a date night with my wife and soulmate, Wendi.

Today, Wendi assists me with research and technology, and she is a truly gifted writer. She has a master's degree in secondary administration and holds three bachelor's degrees in education. She has the same love for kids that I have, and we are both passionate about helping and saving as many kids as possible.

THE HISTORY OF TEEN MURDER

When we examine the history of teen murder, there are a few interesting facts I have discovered. The first case of an American teen murder took place in 1786, when Hannah Occuish, 12, from New London, Connecticut murdered a six-year-old female by strangling and beating her to death with a rock. It started over a dispute about strawberries, and as a punishment for her crime, this 12-year-old child was hanged months later. The first teen thrill killing occurred in 1872 when Jessie Pomeroy killed two male children and tortured six others. His victims ranged in age from four to eight years old, and they were tied up, beaten, and had their throats and genitals slashed. Pomeroy was given a life sentence and spent most of his prison sentence in solitary confinement.

School attacks began in the 1700's, with the first American school attack taking place on July 26, 1764 in Greencastle, Pennsylvania. Named the Enoch Brown School Massacre, ten children were killed and two were injured during the Pontiac War. The school massacre was carried out by four American Indians, who killed the school headmaster, and then slashed and stabbed nine children to death with knives and hatchets, kidnapping some of the children.

Teen murder and school attacks continued into the 1900's, and seemed to pick up in the 1970's, 1980's, and 1990's. The deadliest year for teen murder was 1993, when 3800 teens took the life of another human being. Today, we have approximately 2000 teen murders per year, averaging five to six per day. Along with homicide, thousands of young people take their own lives every year, averaging around 12 per day. Not only are teen school shootings increasing as of late, so is teen suicide, rising 50% in the last several years for female teens, and increasing 30% for male teens, according to a 2008-2015 study conducted by the Centers for Disease Control and Prevention.

When studying teen murder for as long as I have, over the last 35 years, trends can be observed. In the 1980's, Satanism, the Occult and devil worship was a popular trend, and a popular theme in teen entertainment. As well, many music artists and movies promoted these beliefs. Remember Ozzy Osbourne's "Mr. Crowley," Motely Crue's "Shout at the Devil," Van Halen's "Running with the Devil," AC/DC's "Highway to Hell," and Iron Maiden's "The Number of the Beast"? Because teens are influenced and impacted by their culture and their entertainment, the 1980's featured the trend of juvenile satanic killers. Many juvenile murders during this decade had satanic and occult overtones.

The 1990's brought us the introduction of violent video games, and it was no surprise that we saw a new trend of school massacres-shooting and killing multiple people at one time, most of them innocent targets. As the entertainment industry and youth culture continued to promote violence, torture, rape, sodomy and murder, we watched the 2000's become the decade of the family killers. This is the phenomenon of a teen killing everyone, his or her entire family, or as many as he or she could kill at school.

The 2010's were the decade of the female teen killer. There has been an increase of female teen homicides and female teen suicides. Sadly, it is my prediction that in the next decade, the 2020's, we will see the trend of teenagers killing police officers. Our current generation of teens is being taught to not only hate the police, but to systematically kill them. They are being trained in violent video games and they observe the cop-hating culture around them, from the mainstream media to many politicians. The so called "youth entertainment" that teens consume teaches them to shoot, stab, hang and kill police officers.

Before I begin to bring you some of the new research I have completed over the last decade, let me first give you a few basic facts that you should know about teen murder:

1. Juvenile homicide and school shootings are preventable, and most teens have what I call "leakage". They leak violence in their writings, drawings, schoolwork, social media postings, threats, and obsession with guns and violence.

2. Teen killers and school shooters usually plan their crimes for months. Columbine was planned for eighteen months, and Parkland was planned for twelve months. Most plan for at least three to six months, which is why this book and my training is so valuable. Most teen murders and school shootings should have been prevented, and could have, if people knew what to look for. You can't stop teen violence if you don't know the warning signs!

3. 90% of teen killers are male, but we have seen an increase in female teen killers recently, along with female teen suicides.

4. Approximately 2000 of the 12,000 murders in America every year are carried out by teenagers, which averages out to around 5 or 6 per day.

5. Only 10-20% of teens who kill are mentally ill, meaning most teens are not crazy and know what they are doing. Although their brains aren't fully developed until they reach the age of twenty to twenty-five years old, they fully understand that killing people is wrong. They can't fully grasp the consequences they will face after their crime, which is the biggest wake-up call for them.

6. Only 50% of teen killers use guns in the commission of their crimes, and most of them obtain these weapons illegally from their home or a relative's home. What this means is the current gun laws we have in place have little effect on juvenile crime, especially school shootings. This would also apply to gang members and various types of criminals buying illegal or stolen guns. Most murders in the US occur in large cities by gang members and drug dealers who don't obey gun laws.

7. The only profile of a teen killer, in my opinion, is male, since 90% of teen killers are male. After the profile of male, it can be anyone, including any race, any nationality, and of any

socio-economic background. Teen killers and sch◌
white, black, Asian, Hispanic, Alaskan and Native ◌
They are rich, poor, popular, loners, educated, uneducat◌
live in urban, suburban, and rural areas. They are altar b◌
class presidents, valedictorians and Eagle Scouts. As you can
see, they can be anybody, which makes it hard to profile them.
It also makes it vitally important to learn the causes, warning
signs and triggers from my training, so you can learn how to
spot these killers before it's too late.

8. Most school shooters want to die, which makes this type of teen
killer unique due to their suicidal ideologies. Some successfully
kill themselves, and some choose to die by cop. Others decide
during the shooting that they don't have the courage to kill
themselves, while the rest are stopped and apprehended before
they can carry out their suicidal fantasy. School shooters are
one of the few types of teen killers who include suicide as part
of their violent fantasies.

9. The single most common cause of school shootings is bullying,
since nearly every school shooter I have talked to was abused by
classmates or teachers. They feel a need to get revenge, and many
of them just want to die. As of late, they also see the benefit of
becoming famous, which means a lot to those with extremely
low self-esteem, and who have been rejected by females their
whole lives. Thanks to the mainstream media, who makes these
killers household names, they can attain their final wish for
infamy. It should be mentioned that not every country makes
killers famous, especially young killers. In Canada, they shy
away from reporting the names of juvenile killers, which makes
it less appealing when killers don't gain the fame and infamy
from their crimes. Hopefully, we can pass a law in the United
States to make it illegal to mention the name of juvenile killers,
and subsequently decrease the instances of these events.

10. School attacks or massacres occur in all types of schools,
including elementary, middle and high schools, as well as

colleges and universities. They also have taken place in private, public, parochial, urban, suburban, and rural schools.

11. The youngest school shooter that I have discovered so far is a six-year-old male from Flint, Michigan. He brought his uncle's gun to school and killed a female classmate. It was reported that she was teasing him because he was a bedwetter. According to my research through interviewing juvenile killers, bedwetting can be a warning sign of future violence.

12. When a school shooter is carrying out an attack at a school, they will fall into a trance-like state, like they are possessed. Many school killers I interview explain that they don't remember shooting people at their school. Once the killing spree is over, if they survive, a feeling of regret comes over them when they realize what they have done and what potential consequences they will now face, which is most likely a lifetime in prison. They quickly find out that prison is pure hell, and much worse than the bullying and harassment they experienced at school.

13. A teen murder or mass murder can happen anywhere, from a small town to a large city, and in places like a church, a mall, any grade level school, or even a movie theater. Even though the area we live, work or go to school in appears safe, we must never let our guard down. Murder and death can visit us at any time, in any place, when you least expect it. Beautiful towns like Littleton, Colorado and Newtown, Connecticut have unfortunately experienced this harsh reality.

14. Most teen killers and school shooters have no history of violence and usually their first crime is murder or mass murder. Therefore, every threat should be taken seriously, and everyone who displays warning signs should be treated as a potential killer, including elementary school students, special needs students, and students living with the condition of autism.

I hope this answers a few questions you might have about why I do what I do, and some introductory facts about teen murder. We are now ready to move on to explaining why teens kill and how we can stop them. Thanks for reading this book, thanks for your commitment to help children, and thanks for your continued support.

Phil Chalmers
"The Teen Killer Whisperer

CHAPTER ONE
THE SIX TYPES OF TEEN KILLERS

After studying teen killers for 35 years, I have been able to classify them as one of six types. I will describe and provide an example of each, so you can understand how each type of teen killer is different from the other. We typify adult killers into categories such as serial killers, mass murderers and spree killers. Teen killers can also be categorized into six distinct categories, as listed and described below.

THE FAMILY KILLER

I have always found it shocking that a teenager would kill a member of their own family, snuffing out their own flesh and blood. The idea of killing the people who gave them life is against human nature. This killer includes teens who kill their parents, grandparents, siblings, and other relatives. The main causes for these types of murders include loss, abuse, neglect, disagreements, anger, mental illness, or simply for the thrill of it. Sometimes thrill killers murder their own family members because they are the most accessible victims.

CLAY SHROUT

On May 26, 1994, at the age of 17, high school junior Clay Shrout woke up at 5am and walked out to his father's Jeep and grabbed a loaded gun his father kept in his glove compartment. He entered his parents' bedroom where he shot both his father and mother in their heads, killing his mother and wounding his father. He then walked down the hallway of their upscale Florence, Kentucky home and into the bedroom of his sister Kristen, 14, and shot her in the head.

Next, Shrout walked back to his parents' room and explained "My dad was sitting there on the bed...He said something like, "Oh my God"; something to that effect...And I got scared when I saw him, and I fired two more shots at him...After the first shot he just kinda fell over like flat sorta, he was just lying there and there was a weird noise coming from him, like first I thought that he was having trouble breathing. Then I decided it as blood flowing out the hole or something, and that was when I fired the second shot and he was on the ground. I fired that one into the head also." (Kentucky Post, November 6, 1998)

After killing his father, he heard noises from his youngest sister's room, Lauren, age 12. He went into her room, talked to her briefly, and shot her in the head as well. He then got ready for school. When he left for school, he saw a neighbor and announced, "You don't know me...but my name is Clay Shrout and you're going to hear a lot about me today. I'm going to be on CNN," according to the Cincinnati Post, November 7, 1998. He then drove to Danielle's house, a girl he took to prom two weeks earlier, and showed her his gun as he drove her to school.

Shrout walked into his first class at Ryle High School, showed the teacher his gun, and sat down at her desk. He held the teacher, 22 students, and his prom date hostage for ten minutes, until an assistant principal came into the room. A few minutes later the police arrived, and Shrout gave up. Shrout told the police that he killed his family because they took away his weapons due to his low grades. He had intended to kill his English teacher and an assistant principal, but he never accomplished that goal. When asked why he killed his two sisters, he explained "I didn't want them to live without their parents."

In what should have been a warning sign, Shrout took a stun gun to school a few days before killing his family, and the school confiscated it. Shrout came from a stable, church-going family, and both of his parents were Sunday school teachers. He was not a loner and had plenty of friends, and did fairly well in school. He did change the last year or two prior to the murders, wearing all black, using drugs and alcohol, and reportedly talking about killing people. He was obsessed with weapons, and had a small collection of knives, death stars and a sword. He was also studying how to build bombs, and he had an interest in the occult, vampires and Satanism. He read satanic books and had dark posters on his bedroom walls. He was also a self- abuser, talked about suicide, and was abusive toward his family dogs.

When asked why he had to kill his parents, he explained that he wanted to run away but he knew they would stop him. The real reason is he didn't like being disciplined. Because of his recent suspension for bringing his stun gun to school, as well as his dropping grades, his parents grounded him and took away his collection of weapons, his heavy metal music and his computer, according to the Cincinnati Enquirer, May 25, 2004. Another warning sign was a drawing Shrout made of his assistant principal tied to a pole with gasoline poured around him, apparently because he was mad at him for taking his weapon. He also asked a friend what the best way was to kill someone, and the friend was concerned and asked Clay if he was planning on killing his parents. Shrout responded "No, but my parents are kind of just getting in the way." (Associated Press, May 27, 2004).

One of the arresting officers explained "He's probably the darkest person I've come into contact with…He showed no emotion. He was so matter of fact." (Kentucky Post, May 26, 2004). He pleaded guilty by reason of insanity and was sentenced to 25 years to life. He will be eligible for parole in 2019. We had communicated in the past, but with his possible parole nearing, he probably had been advised to not talk to people like me by his attorneys, since it might jeopardize his release.

JOSHUA COOKE

Joshua Cooke, 19, was obsessed with violence, and was overly fixated on his favorite movie, The Matrix. He tried to emulate the characters in the film, dressed like them, and even bought a gun that resembled the one used in the movie.

On February 17, 2003, in Fairfax, Virginia, Joshua was helping his adoptive parents by shoveling snow. He even helped his neighbors and shoveled their driveway as well. After doing his chores, he escaped into his world of violent video games, as he did many nights. Later that evening, he was ready to carry out his murderous fantasy. After dinner, and angry at his adoptive parents, he grabbed his shotgun, looked up at the Matrix poster in his bedroom, and put on his music headphones. He was listening to the band Drowning Pool, and their song "Bodies," which includes the line "Let the bodies hit the floor." He decided it was time to end his parents' lives, and his own life as well. Cooke told Piers Morgan "I wanted to end my life and theirs."

Joshua walked down to the basement, and as his mother turned to him from her computer, he shot her in the chest. He then opened fire on his father, shooting him six times as he hid under a desk, all while his father was on the phone with his sister. He walked back upstairs to his bedroom to reload his shotgun and returned to the basement. His mother was not dead, and instead, clutched the hole in her chest, asking Josh why he shot her. He then shot her in the face, killing her, and then finished his father off with one last shot to the head.

He explained "I was numb. There had been so many years of hurt from my mother's abuse and bullying, rejection from girls, all types of things like that. I just didn't care about anything anymore." He also considered opening fire at his school, but instead, sat on the front porch drinking a soda and called police, telling them "I just shot my parents, just blew them away with a shotgun." Cooke later explained he was angry at his parents, he had been suicidal and felt he was mentally ill. He had been abandoned by his parents who were both paranoid schizophrenics, and he was a ward of the state until he and his sister were adopted by the Virginia couple when Joshua was six-years old. The police found numerous disturbing items in his bedroom, including information about serial killers and the death penalty. He was convicted of both murders and sentenced to 40 years in prison.

TYLER HADLEY

On July 16, 2011, Tyler Hadley, 17, killed his parents with a hammer, and spent the next three hours cleaning up the blood. He lived in Port St Lucie, Florida with his parents, Blake and Mary Jo. They were very strict with him, and there was constant friction between the three. Tyler had been seeing a psychologist and was also taking medications. All week at school, Tyler bragged that he was having a party, but nobody believed him. He began posting on the day of the murder that he might have a party, and finally, after killing his parents, posted on his social media page that he was definitely having a party.

After Hadley killed his parents and cleaned up, he went to an ATM and removed $5000 from his parents' bank account, and picked up some friends on the way back home to his party. While high on Ecstasy, he and sixty guests partied in the home within feet of his parents' dead bodies, which were stacked on top of each other in the master bedroom. They drank, smoked cigars, and played beer pong. Hadley was planning a second party the next night, but after showing one of his friends the dead bodies, the friend called police and he was arrested the following morning.

Hadley claimed he was abused, but from reports and research, it was reported that there was no truth to that. Tyler's brother Ryan claimed that his parents were great people, and his brother Tyler was a pathological liar. Tyler told me that along with using drugs, he was a fan of violent music and a music group called Insane Clown Posse. A fellow inmate said that Hadley had signed autographs in prison, called himself "hammer boy" and claims that he has talked to the devil. When Tyler was ten, he told a friend that he wanted to kill his parents. After the actual murder of his parents, he was arrested and found guilty of two counts of first-degree murder and sentenced to life without parole.

THE SCHOOL KILLER

The media buzzword "school shooter" gets a lot of attention today and assures the media of stellar ratings with millions of transfixed eyes glued to each detail in every single one of these events. Instead of school shooters, as the mainstream media refers to them, I call them what they really are-school killers. School attacks have been around since 1764 in the United States, and believe it or not, we have had school shootings in just about every decade since 1920. They started to become more frequent in the 1970's and 1980's, with the rise of drug use, suicide, and Satanism among youth. But school shootings changed with the advent of violent, first-person shooter video games being released in the early 1990's. After the release of this violent entertainment, and with the consumption of this material by youth and children, we observed a new phenomenon-school massacres. Students walking into schools and killing multiple people, mostly innocent victims. No matter how long you look at research, you will find very few mass shootings with multiple deaths by a juvenile in the United States prior to 1992. The two exceptions are the sniper style shooting by Anthony Barbaro in 1975 in New York, and the Brenda Spencer sniper style shooting in San Diego in 1979.

With the release of first-person shooter video games like Doom, Duke Nukem, and Grand Theft Auto, beginning in 1992, school shootings transformed. Not only did we see an increase of school shootings every year, but we saw an increase in victims per shooting. The average number of victims of a school shooting rose from 1-2 in prior decades, to an average of 5 victims per incident. In a sense, it became a mass shooting and the victims were almost all random, innocent targets. In our current decade, 2010 to 2019, we have seen more school shootings than ever before, and we have never seen so many victims shot and stabbed in one decade. In a later chapter, I will share with you the numbers and details of school shootings by decade, and at the end of this book will be the longest list of school shootings by teens ever assembled.

School killers are one of the few types of teen killers who want to die during their crime, along with family killers and thrill killers. Suicide is a very big part of their fantasy of being a mass killer and going out in a blaze of glory.

NIKOLAS CRUZ, FEBRUARY 14, 2018

On February 14, 2018, Valentine's Day, 19-year-old Nikolas Cruz carried out the deadliest school shooting in 2018, and one of the deadliest of all time. With Columbine being the benchmark of school shootings for nearly twenty years, expelled student Cruz took an Uber to school and hid his rifle in a black bag. He walked into Marjory Stoneman Douglas High School and headed for a stairway. A freshman student walked in on him, as he was removing his rifle from his bag, and he told the student to get out of there because something bad was about to happen. A teacher then confronted him, and he shot and killed the teacher. He moved from floor to floor, shooting victims on two of the three floors of the building. Some were shot in the hallways, and some were shot in classrooms from broken door windows. He was able to kill seventeen students and teachers, and wounded another seventeen.

Sadly, Nikolas Cruz is a poster boy for school killers, displaying almost every cause and warning sign in my book. In addition, he was motivated by multiple triggers, including being expelled from school, and rejected by his love interest. In his interview with police, he talked about his fascination with guns and explained how he legally purchased multiple rifles and pellet guns. He also talked about killing animals, experiencing demons, the voices in his head, his drug use, and his desire to kill himself. He had been posting pictures on social media of him with his guns and knives, and he had posted that he wanted to be a "professional school shooter" someday.

He claimed he owned three rifles, three shotguns, including an AK-47 and an AR-15. He said he kept the guns in a gun safe at his friend's home, where he was living at the time. He and his brother were in foster care, but his foster parents had since died, so he was staying with a friend.

After the murder spree he dropped his rifle and one hundred and eighty live rounds and walked out of the building with the rest of the students, and later visited McDonalds and Walmart, grabbing a drink before he was arrested. Some of his victims were shot multiple times, as he came back and shot wounded students, killing them. The police officer assigned to the school waited outside the school and never entered the building, and it took another law enforcement agency to arrive and enter the building eleven minutes into the shooting. When the officers entered the building, the local deputies followed them in. This gave Cruz plenty of time to carry out his crime spree, having shot thirty four people in six minutes, before exiting the building. I'm sure he was surprised by how much time he had, probably expecting to be killed by the school resource officer in the first few minutes. As of the writing of this book, Cruz is awaiting trial, possibly facing the death penalty, and is on 24-hour suicide watch. He is famous like the rest of his school shooter peers and gets hundreds of pieces of mail at the jail, including marriage proposals, nude photos and funds for his commissary account.

CHARLES ANDREW WILLIAMS

On March 5, 2001, Charles "Andy" Williams, 15, opened fire at Santana High School in Santee, California, shooting fifteen fellow students, killing two. The weapon he used was a .22 caliber revolver he stole from his father, and bullying was the main cause of his rampage. Andy was born in Maryland, and when his parents split up, he and his father moved to California, where the incessant bullying began. After months of constant bullying, Williams made a statement that he "didn't want to live anymore." When one of his teachers humiliated him in front of his class, it was the last straw. It was reported that Williams told friends a few times that he wanted to "pull a Columbine," but nobody ever reported it. Not only was he planning on shooting his bullies, but he also wanted to get on top of the school, to have a better chance of killing from a bird's eye view.

Williams had been planning his murderous shooting over the weekend, and on Monday, March 5, he made his plan a reality. He entered the boys' bathroom in the morning and shot and killed a male freshman student. He then exited the bathroom and began firing at multiple students, killing one more, and injuring thirteen others. As the students ran and ducked for cover, he walked back into the bathroom after he ran out of ammo, to reload. A campus security officer and a student teacher walked into the bathroom, not knowing the gunman was in there, and both were shot multiple times by Williams. Thankfully, both survived.

Some of the witnesses said they had seen Andy Williams smiling during the killing spree. A little later, the police and swat team finally entered the bathroom and found Williams kneeling on the floor, wanting to kill himself, but he didn't have the courage to do it. In the end, eleven students were shot and injured, as well as two adult staff members. Two students died, including a fourteen-year-old male and a seventeen-year-old male. After the incident, over seventy students admitted that they knew Williams was going to shoot up the school on Monday.

Andy was a fan of the popular alternative rock band, Linkin Park, and his note to his father included some of his favorite band's lyrics. The note read "I tried so hard, and got so far, but in the end it doesn't really matter." These words include lyrics from Linkin Park's song "In the End." The song "One Step Closer" includes the lyrics "I'm one step closer to the edge, and I'm about to break." Williams also cited his parents' divorce as a contributor, along with his abrupt move across the country, suicidal thoughts, and the death of a friend. After his arrest, he told police that "he was tired of being bullied." Williams had his backpack ripped off, thrown in the trash and he had salad dressing poured on top of him. On Friday, a teacher embarrassed him in front of the class, calling him stupid, and he explained to me this would act as a trigger for the murderous event. He explained, "I was bullied, I was sexually assaulted by my friend's step-dad, I was called names. I believed everyone hated me, so I began to hate myself." Williams was sentenced to life in prison and could be eligible for parole in 5 years.

THE TEN MYTHS OF A SCHOOL SHOOTER

Myth Number One: They didn't fit the profile: Truth: There is no profile, except male. 90% of school shooters and teen killers are male.

Myth Number Two: They snapped. Truth: Teen killers and school shooters never snap, they plan for six months, twelve months, and longer. Columbine was planned for eighteen months.

Myth Number Three: Nobody knew their plans. Truth: School shooters display plenty of warning signs and can rarely contain their violent plans. I call it leakage, when their violence begins to leak out, in words, threats, drawings, social media posts, poetry, artwork, and more. Also, school shooters do tell people, and most likely at least one or more of their friends or classmates knew something was planned.

Myth Number Four: They didn't threaten anyone. Truth: Most school shooters don't make direct threats, but instead make more general statements of feeling wronged and wanting revenge.

Myth Number Five: They are all loners. Truth: School shooters and teen killers are sometimes popular, having friends, girlfriends, and are sometimes successful in sports and involved in school clubs and activities.

Myth Number Six: They are all crazy. Truth: Although people use mental illness as the last resort to explain why young people want to kill others, the majority of teen killers and school shooters are not mentally ill. Mental illness is one of the least common causes of teen murder, with only 10-20% of school shooters being diagnosed as mentally ill.

Myth Number Seven: If only the police had showed up quicker. Truth: Most school shootings are over in six to eight minutes, which is about as long as it would take for police officers to arrive on the scene. Sandy Hook was over in six minutes, and Kip Kinkel shot over 50 rounds in Springfield, Oregon in three minutes. At Parkland, Florida, the shooter's killing spree was over in four minutes, as 34 people were shot. Unless you have a police officer assigned to your school, the chances of responding police officers stopping the incident are very low. Most first responders to these shootings are teachers, coaches, principals, and students.

Myth Number Eight: If we can ban AR-15's, we can stop school shootings. Truth: The deadliness of a school shooting is not determined by the gun used, but instead, is dependent on the amount of time the killer has, and how accessible his victims are. If a school shooting lasts longer than three minutes, there will be a higher number of victims. If the shooting ends quickly, like the 2005 Maryland school shooting, which was over in 90 seconds, the body count will be low. The shooting in Maryland had only one death, and it was the shooter, who was killed by police in 90 seconds.

The school killers with the highest body count had plenty of time to carry out their murderous fantasies. These include Virginia Tech, Sandy Hook, Parkland, and Santa Fe, Texas. In reference to the weapon used, the third deadliest mass shooting in American history is Virginia Tech, with the killer using two small handguns to carry out his killing spree. Virginia Tech is the deadliest school shooting of all grade level schools in American history.

Regarding ease of access to victims, I advocate that schools not only lock their exterior doors, but also always keep their classroom doors locked, essentially being in "lock down" every hour. This prevents killers from trapping and killing students in unlocked classrooms. The deadliest school shootings had unlocked doors, including Virginia Tech, Sandy Hook, and Santa Fe, Texas. Parkland had locked doors, but easily breakable door glass.

Myth Number Nine: The school did everything they could. Truth: Most schools are not doing everything they can, and many are still in denial. Many schools don't take bullying seriously, and most don't spend the money needed to secure their buildings. Many schools still don't have a police officer assigned to their school buildings, and most don't have classroom doors that lock from the inside. Many schools around the country, including Florida, have doors that must be locked from the hallway with a key, meaning you have to walk outside of the classroom during a shooting and place yourself in harms' way to secure your classroom, if the school doesn't require teachers to have their doors locked at all times during the school day. Sandy Hook Elementary had doors that only locked from the outside, and it was rumored that most of the teachers didn't even know where the keys to their doors were located. Virginia Tech took it a step further and had classroom doors with no locks at all.

Myth Number Ten: School shootings are rampant. Truth: Although the media makes it seem like there are school shootings happening every week, the fact is they are rare. On average, we have approximately five to ten school shootings every school year, and with the amount of schools that are in the United States, approximately 115,000, the chance of a school shooting happening at your school is extremely low. Suicide is much more prevalent, especially female suicides. Even though these incidents are rare, it is wise to be proactive and prepared. Also, hundreds of school shootings have been prevented because of law enforcement, school administrators, teachers, and students who have reported the warning signs of violence. I love these sayings: For students, "If you see something, say something." For adults, "You can't stop violence when you don't know the warning signs."

FAME AND CELEBRITY

Many teen killers and school shooters crave fame, and the mainstream media delivers. Because the mainstream media needs viewers, they know that school shootings and mass murders will bring them great ratings, with millions of eyeballs watching. What they don't understand is future school shooters and mass murderers are watching as well. Major media outlets and major newspapers and magazines, along with thousands of local news stations and local newspapers all blame a myriad of people and organizations for school shootings, all the while putting out a casting call for the next school shooter. Unfortunately, school shooters and mass murderers are their stars, and business is good.

In case you didn't know, there are countries like Canada that don't allow the media to make killers famous, legally forbidding them to mention juvenile killers' names. As one of the main solutions to school killings, we need to make it illegal for the news media to make juvenile killers famous, making it illegal to mention their names, and encouraging them to stop talking about these killers and incidents for days, weeks and months. Let's stop making killers famous, and instead, focus on the victims and the heroes who stop these incidents. By doing this, we can stop juveniles who are wanting to be, as Nikolas Cruz boasted in his Twitter post "a professional school shooter".

THE GANG/CULT KILLER

The gang killer is inspired and motivated by the gang he or she is in, the color he or she wears, or the block they represent. The gang can be a localized gang, or major national gang like the Bloods, Crips or MS-13. The cult killer is motivated or inspired by the belief system of their sect, and could be groups like the white supremacists, Satanists, or the Juggalos, who are fans of an old school rap group called Insane Clown Posse, also known as ICP. These people are so entrenched in their gangs and cults that they are willing to break laws to support the message of their groups, including taking other people's lives.

NATHAN BROOKS

On September 30, 1995, approaching Halloween season, Nathan Brooks, 17, from Bellaire, Ohio, committed an unspeakable crime, turning his home into a house of horrors. It was the year trick-or-treat was cancelled, and there was no candy for the kids. Nathan had been an altar boy and had dreams of someday being a priest. But his babysitter turned him on to satanic music, like Slayer and Cannibal Corpse, and the occult. So, he did a complete turnaround from religion and decided to be the best Satanist he could be. And for him, it was breaking all Ten Commandments.

Nathan told me that nine of the Ten Commandments were easy, but the last one, "Thou shalt not kill" would be the most difficult. He assembled a hit list of thirteen names, beginning with his own brother, his mother, his father, and his Catholic priest. The rest of the list were members of the community. Next to some of the names were the words "molest," "skin," "decapitate," and "eviscerate." He wanted to complete the list by killing himself. He felt this would please Satan and would make him a great Satanist. He also built a satanic altar in his bedroom, complete with a satanic bible, candle, knife, and a load of satanic drawings, artwork and poetry. For some reason, his parents were not concerned. So, on Saturday night, he began his killing spree.

His brother, Ryan, 16, ended up not coming home, so he survived this murderous night. His next two victims on his list were his parents. They slept in separate bedrooms, so he decided to kill his mother, Marylyn, 52, first. He smashed her head with an axe, knocking her out. And then he stabbed her repeatedly, leaving the knife in her body. He was going to crucify her to the wall but could not pick her up. He then grabbed his father's hunting rifle, and as he stood at the doorway of 53-year-old Terry's bedroom, shot him three times in the head. Then, he retrieved a hacksaw, cut his father's head off, placed it in a punch bowl on top of his satanic altar, and performed a satanic ceremony. He left his house and took off to kill the priest that he worked for, but he got held up, and arrested later that night.

When Brooks was arrested, he told Sheriff Tom McCort "People don't understand." He confessed to the crimes, was convicted and sentenced to life in prison, and will spend the rest of his natural life in there. When I met with Nathan, he told me he no longer believed in Satan, but thought the reason he did the crimes was because, "Satan was my father, and I was willing to do anything to please my father... rape, torture, murder, and even kill myself." He won't be eligible for parole until 2038.

ROD FERRELL

On November 25, 1996, the week of Thanksgiving, Roderick Ferrell, 17, and his "Vampire Clan" carried out a vicious double murder in Eustis, Florida. Rod and his co-conspirator, Howard Scott Anderson, entered the home of Heather Wendorf's parents, who was one of Rod's good friends. Rod, using a crow bar, beat Mr. Wendorf to death as he slept on the couch. He was then confronted by Mrs. Wendorf, who had just emerged from the shower. She threw a hot cup of coffee on him, so he proceeded to beat her to death with the crow bar as well. After killing the couple, Rod, Howard, Heather, Rod's girlfriend Charity and Dana fled the area and headed toward New Orleans. Charity had placed a phone call to her mother in an attempt to get money, but her mother called the police and provided them with her daughter's whereabouts, leading to the arrest of the Vampire Clan.

Born in Murray, Kentucky, Ferrell was raised by a single mother who allowed him to experiment with violent movies, the occult, and vampire activities. Ferrell would tell people that he was a 500-year-old vampire named Vesago, a character he created for the game he liked to play with his friends, Vampire the Masquerade.

Originally sentenced to death in 1998, Ferrell was one of the youngest people on death row for two years, when his sentence was commuted to life without parole. He has been trying to obtain a new trial to eventually win parole and his release from prison, but to date, it has been denied. A movie was made about the crime in 2002, called Vampire Clan. I had the opportunity to interview Rod for the show Crime Watch Daily, and he was friendly and cordial to me and my team.

THE CRIME KILLER

This killer didn't wake up with a plan to take someone's life, but because of the criminal activity that they are involved in, a murder occurred, and someone lost their life. This could include drug deals gone bad, the rape that turns into a murder, and a robbery or burglary that turns deadly.

DEVIN THOMPSON

Devin Moore, 18, was arrested on June 7, 2003, on suspicion of stealing a car in Fayette, Alabama, by the Fayette Police Department. While he was being processed and booked, the Fayette police officer took him lightly because he knew him, removing his handcuffs, and not locking up his weapon. Thompson waited for the right opportunity and grabbed Officer Strickland's gun, shooting him multiple times and killing him. Next, he exited the booking room and shot Sargent James Crump in the head, and when he went down, shot him multiple times, killing him. He then walked into the dispatcher's office and shot and killed dispatcher Mealer, shooting him in the head. He killed the entire police department that day, as only three employees were in the office. He considered killing the entire fire department, which is physically attached to the police department, but for some reason, he decided against that.

Devin was a violent gamer, and Grand Theft Auto was his favorite game, which glamorizes numerous street crimes, including stealing cars and police cars, and killing cops. Just like his game, Thompson stole a police car after his murder rampage, and went on a two-hour joy ride. He was apprehended in Mississippi by the local authorities, and his statement to the police was cold and shocking. "Life is like a video game...everyone has to die sometime." He also told arresting officers that he did it and he killed the police officers because he didn't want to go to jail. Moore had just enlisted in the Air Force and was preparing to leave to serve his country. He had never been in trouble before, and his brother was a successful college football player.

This caused a major controversy with the violent video game Grand Theft Auto, resulting in a lawsuit. The case and crime were featured on 60 Minutes on March 4, 2005. Thompson pleaded not guilty, and his attorneys talked about the violent video game and his abusive father in their defense strategy. Moore was convicted of the three murders, and in 2005, was sentenced to death by lethal injection. So far, all his appeals have been denied, and as of this writing, he remains on Alabama's death row.

CHRISTINE PAOLILLA

On July 18, 2003, in Clear Lake City, Texas, Christine Paolilla, 17, and her boyfriend Christopher Snider went to a home with a plan to steal drugs, and in the process of the armed robbery, Snider and Paolilla shot and killed all four of the home's occupants, two being friends of Paolilla. Known as "The Clear Lake Murders," this case has been featured on numerous television shows, including "Killer Kids," "20/20," "Forensic Files," "Snapped" and "Deadly Women."

The victims were Marcus Precella, Adelbert Sanchez, Tiffany Towell and Rachael Koloroutis, and they were shot and killed with two small caliber handguns. Towell and Koloroutis were friends of Paolilla, and Paolilla helped kill her friend Koloroutis, pistol whipping her in the head, as she tried to crawl to a phone to call police. She also shot at least one more of the four victims. The male victims sold drugs out of the home, and they were the target of the robbery.

Paolilla was raised in a very unstable home, as her father was killed at work when she was only two-years old. Her mother was a drug addict, and eventually lost her children, causing Christine to move in with her grandparents. Paolilla also suffered with some health problems in school, which caused her to be bullied.

Snider and Paolilla were able to get away with the crime for three years, but Paolilla was arrested on July 19, 2006, in a San Antonio, Texas hotel room with her husband Stanley Rott, a heroin addict. Snider committed suicide in Greenville, South Carolina, overdosing on medication. His body was found on August 5, 2006.

Paolilla was convicted of four counts of capital murder on October 13, 2008. Because she was a juvenile, she did not qualify for the death penalty. Paolilla was sentenced to life in prison with a chance at parole in 38 years but has lost all her appeals so far.

THE BABY KILLER

These killers are usually young ladies who are not allowed to date, or not allowed to be sexually active. Most are afraid of their parents and don't want to disappoint them. So, when they find out they are pregnant, instead of having an abortion, they carry the baby full term, usually wearing loose clothing to hide their pregnancy. After giving birth to the baby, usually at home or at school, they stab or strangle the baby to death. They often throw the baby's body in the trash or hide it in their home. Some bury the baby in their backyard.

CASSIDY GOODSON

On September 19, 2012, 14-year-old Cassidy Goodson gave birth to a baby boy in Greenbrier Village, Florida, then strangled him to death. She had hidden her pregnancy from her parents because she explained "I was just scared that our relationship with my family, my parents would not be the same."

Goodson explained that she gave birth to the baby in the bathroom and strangled the full-term child to death. She then placed the infant's body inside a plastic bag and hid it in a shoe box in her bedroom. She was facing adult charges of first-degree murder and aggravated child abuse, but she pleaded guilty to a lesser charge of manslaughter and was sentenced to only 18 months in prison. She explained why she killed the child, stating "I wanted it to stop breathing so I wouldn't get in trouble."

ASHLEY MARIE REED

In June of 2014, Ashley Marie Reed, 16, from Louisburg, North Carolina killed her baby girl, placed her dead body into a garbage bag and buried the dead body of the baby in her parents' backyard. She hid her pregnancy from her parents the entire time, being afraid of what they would do to her. The cause of death for the baby was that it bled to death, due to her cutting the umbilical cord too close to the body. She was sentenced to community service.

THE THRILL KILLER

Like a serial killer, the teen thrill killer has a need or fantasy to commit murder. Their desire to know what it's like to take another person's life is so strong that they plan and go through with it. The most famous teen thrill killer in American history is Jeffrey Dahmer, who kidnaped and killed a male hitchhiker in Bath, Ohio when he was seventeen. Unlike most teens, he was able to get away with his murder and couldn't stop the urge to kill again. Thankfully, most teen thrill killers are caught and stopped after their first homicide.

MONTIE RISSELL

Monte was a troubled child and committed his first rape at the age of 14, and by the age of 19, he had successfully killed five women and raped at least 12 others. His first murder victim was a prostitute he killed during sex, in which he liked to control his victims. She fought back against his violent and aggressive behavior and ran away. He chased her down into a ravine, choked her, bashed her head against a rock, and drowned her in the river. His five murders occurred during the years of 1976 and 1977, and his first murder in 1976 was triggered by the anger and rage he experienced when he saw his ex-girlfriend with her new boyfriend. He usually carried out his rapes and murders when he was high and drunk, which fueled his hate and anger against women. He was arrested in 1978, convicted, and sentenced to five life sentences.

As in the typical killer upbringing, he experienced turmoil and instability. His parents split up when he was seven years old, and although he begged to live with his father, he never saw him again. By the age nine he was already displaying troubling behavior, including writing obscene graffiti on his school's walls and shooting his cousin with a bb gun. His troubles continued as his first burglary occurred when he was twelve, and at the age of thirteen he was arrested for driving without a license. At fourteen, he was arrested for stealing a car, as well as the rape and robbery of a neighbor.

Fueled by his hatred for women and a bad relationship with his own mother, he went on to kill four female victims in the Alexandria, Virginia area. He said one of the victims talked too much, so he raped her and stabbed her to death. He described how the women made him so mad he would see red, which was the best way to describe his rage and anger. He allowed one of the victims to live because he felt sorry for her since she was caring for her grandfather, who was dying of cancer. The last two victims were killed violently, one being drowned and the other being stabbed over 100 times. Rissell was convicted and sentenced to life in prison, and was one of the killers the FBI Profilers interviewed in their study of violent killers. He was also one of the killers featured in the first season of Netflix's Mindhunter series.

HARVEY ROBINSON

Allentown, Pennsylvania was a safe town with relatively little crime, but that all changed in the summer of 1992 when teenager Harvey Robinson's crime spree began. For the first time, Allentown, Pennsylvania was being stalked by a serial killer. Harvey grew up in a troubled home, with his father being an alcoholic and abusive to his mother. By the time Harvey turned three-years-old, his parents were already divorced. His father finally ended up going to prison for beating his girlfriend to death, but no matter what his father did, Harvey Jr worshipped his father, also named Harvey.

As young Harvey grew up, he excelled in sports and academic studies, but he also had a dark side that concerned others. By the age of nine, school counselors determined that young Harvey had a severe conduct disorder, and he would often find himself in trouble between the ages of nine and seventeen years old, arrested for numerous crimes including burglary and resisting arrest. He also was a drug user which helped fuel his violence and anger. As Harvey grew older and began threatening those around him, he was feared by teachers, students and even the police.

Harvey upped his criminal behavior on August 9, 1992, when at the age of seventeen, he began his rape and killing spree. One day earlier, he broke into the home of a 29-year-old female and stole $50. The next day he came back, raped and beat her to death, hitting her on the head over 30 times, fracturing her skull. He killed again on June 9, 1993, kidnapping, raping and stabbing a fifteen-year-old female to death. The young girl disappeared as she was delivering newspapers on her early morning route. Evidence showed that she was raped, stabbed 22 times and her throat had been cut. Eight days later, on June 17, 1993, Harvey's crime spree continued as he burglarized a nearby home and stole the owners gun collection.

On June 20, 1993, Robinson struck again, entering another woman's home. He raped and choked her five-year-old daughter, and attempted to kill her, but luckily, she survived. The police theorized that his targeted victim was the little girl's mother, but she was sleeping with someone at the time. Once again just eight days later, on June 28, Robinson raped a female victim and then attempted to kill her, but he was interrupted by a neighbor. She survived the attack but was severely beaten and had been strangled.

On July 14, 1993, Robinson raped and murdered a 47-year-old female in her daughter's home. The victim was found partially clothed with a swollen face. She had been raped, strangled and savagely beaten. The victim's granddaughter witnessed the attack and was able to provide authorities a description of the killer. A short time later, Robinson returned to the home of the victim who survived, but the police predicted he would do that and were staked out at her home. There was a scuffle and an exchange of gunfire, but Robinson escaped although he did have a gunshot wound. When he visited the hospital to get his bullet wound treated, he was arrested, and his serial crime spree came to an end.

Robinson was charged and found guilty of burglary, kidnapping, rape, and murder. He was initially given three death sentences, but so far has been able to overturn two of the three death sentences, which were commuted to life without parole. He will likely spend the rest of his natural life behind bars.

KENNY LOGGINS, TRACE DUNCAN, CAREY DALE GRAYSON, LOUIS MANGIONE

On February 22, 1994, in Trussville, Alabama, Vicki Lynn DeBlieux was hitchhiking, trying to get from Chattanooga, Tennessee to West Monroe, Louisiana. She was given a ride by Kenny Loggins, 17, Trace Duncan, 17, Carey Dale Grayson, 19, and Louis Mangione, 17. The four young men kidnapped, raped and beat her so badly that every bone in her head was broken. They stood on her throat and Duncan inserted a beer bottle into her vagina and kicked it inside her. After they killed Vicki, whom they called "the perfect victim," they tossed her dead body into a dump in St Clair County.

After the murder, the group of boys dropped off Mangione, and returned to the scene with knives, and began to stab the dead woman. She was stabbed over 180 times, and her body had been grotesquely cut open. They took bites of her flesh and tasted her interior organs, and then cut off all of her fingers to take home as trophies. They removed one of her lungs, and Grayson and Loggins took a bite of it. Loggins then spit his mouthful of her lung into her face. They gave one of the dead girl's fingers to Mangione, who showed a friend, leading to the four killers' arrest.

Grayson came from a troubled home and his parents divorced and he later dropped out of school after his mother was killed when he was only twelve-years-old. Grayson also suffered with manic depression, which was reported as a family disease. Loggins was abandoned by both parents at an early age and began using drugs at the age of 13. Loggins also suffered from depression, was suicidal, and was harming himself.

All four boys were convicted of the murder, and Loggins, Grayson and Duncan were sentenced to death by electric chair. Mangione was given a lesser sentence of life without parole. Because Loggins and

Duncan were juveniles at the time of the murder, their death sentences were commuted to life without parole.

ALYSSA BUSTAMANTE

Alyssa Bustamante, from Jefferson City, Missouri, seemed like a typical fifteen-year-old girl. She enjoyed hanging out with friends and spending time with her siblings. But she also seemed to push the boundaries, wearing her hatchet necklace, posting photos on social media of her pretending to stab another student in the school cafeteria, and encouraging others to touch an electric fence while she videotaped them. She also took photos for social media meant to shock others, pretending to shoot herself and with blood dripping out of her mouth. She came from a troubled home with a history of drug use and suicide attempts, had no father, and lived with her grandmother.

Alyssa kept a journal of her thoughts and fantasies and would repeatedly write that if she didn't get help, she would eventually kill someone because of the rage that had built up insider her. She also wanted to know what it felt like to kill another human being. On October 21, 2009, she decided to fulfill her fantasy of death and murder. She lured her neighbor, nine-year-old Elizabeth Olten to a wooded area behind their homes, where she had already dug a grave. She made the little girl lay down in the grave and then she attacked. She stabbed the child in the chest, strangled her, slit her wrists, cut her throat, and unbuttoned her pants, before she buried her dead body and covered her with leaves. Alyssa had dug two graves, and it was thought that she might have had plans to kill her two little brothers.

She wrote in her journal next to her bed "I just fucking killed someone. I strangled them and slit their throat and stabbed them and now they're dead. I don't know how to feel at the moment, it was ahmazing. As soon as you get over the 'ohmygawd I can't do this feeling,' it's pretty enjoyable. I'm kinda nervous and shaky though right now. Kay, I gotta go to church now...lol." On one of her social media profiles, she listed "killing people" as one of her hobbies. At the same time, she attended the local Mormon Church and was involved in the youth group. She had attempted suicide multiple times, was a cutter and was on medication. Alyssa was born to a teenage mother who had numerous brushes with the law. Her father was serving a ten-year sentence for assault.

A letter led police to Alyssa, and she quickly confessed and led authorities to the body of her victim. She was arrested and convicted of second-degree murder in 2012 and sentenced to life in prison with the possibility of parole. Her reason for doing it was simple-she wanted to know what it felt like to kill someone.

CHAPTER TWO
THE CAUSES OF TEEN MURDER

Teen murder and school shootings are what I call "multiple cause" crimes, meaning it takes more than one cause to create a teen killer and school shooter. In my research, it usually takes between three and six causes. Some people will pull out one of my causes and argue that you can't blame a teen murder on a single cause such as a video game, bullying or poverty. But they don't understand my stance, or my philosophy about a multiple cause crime. I agree with them; their point that you can't blame video games alone for school shootings or teen murder. But I am fully convinced that every cause that I list plays a part in the creation of teen killers and school shooters.

If you are a parent, please examine this list of causes, and ask yourself, how many of these listed does my child have in his or her life? If it is just one or two, you should be ok. If there are three to six or more causes that your child exhibits, he or she is in the danger zone. That still doesn't mean he or she is going to be a killer, but possesses the components of a possible killer depending on what happens in his or her life, and the kind of circumstances and triggers encountered. So, as an example, if your son comes from a divorced home and plays Grand Theft Auto, and everything else is stable, you should be fine. If your daughter has no father-figure in her life and loves guns, but everything else is stable, you are more than likely safe. But if your son loves guns, Grand Theft Auto, is wetting the bed in his adolescence, your cat is missing, and your shed just burned down, Holy Shit! You see what I am saying…it is not just one cause, or one single factor.

I ranked the causes, just as I have observed and recorded them, with the number one cause being the most common I see, and number thirteen being the least common. And yes, mental illness is one of the least common causes. When the "so called" experts run out of the reasons why teens kill, or they just don't understand, or they usually conclude that all teen killers must be mentally ill. Unfortunately, this is not an easy problem to solve. And most teen killers and school shooters are not mentally ill. The opposite is true.…most know exactly what they are doing, and they definitely know it's wrong.

CAUSE NUMBER ONE-FATHERLESSNESS

After researching thousands of cases, and interviewing hundreds of killers personally, I have come to the overwhelming conclusion that the number one cause of teen murder is no father, or in reality, no daddy. I have the advantage of interviewing all types of killers, from teen killers to school shooters, and mass murderers to serial killers. The single connection they all have is no healthy father figure. Most of the killers have mothers and grandmothers, but few have a daddy. And if they have a father, most of their fathers end up being bad guys. At a minimum, killers had fathers who were absent and uninterested in their children's lives. Dad, I'm speaking directly to you: Please don't make this mistake! And Mom, if your children don't have an active father, please make sure they have a positive male influence in their lives, be it a grandfather, an uncle, or a positive male role model like a coach.

As you read though the rest of this book, you will observe that most of the killers that fill these pages are being raised by a mother, a grandmother or even a friend's parents. Thrill killer Alyssa Bustamante lived with her grandparents, and family killer Holly Harvey lived with her drug-addicted mother and then was taken in by her grandparents. School shooter Luke Woodham from Pearl, Mississippi lived with his single mother, while the Parkland, Florida school shooter lived with a friend's family. You might also observe that if these teen killers or school shooters did have a father, there seemed to be a strained relationship, and these kids seemed to have a perceived wrong. This by far is the number one cause of teen killers, and like I always say, "show me a teen killer, and I will show you a kid who doesn't have a daddy."

CAUSE NUMBER TWO-UNSTABLE HOME AND ABUSE

Fifty percent of children grow up in broken homes, living with one parent or the other. In some urban areas, this number has climbed to eighty percent and higher. This also includes a divorced home with the parents playing games and using their children as pawns, being a "Disney Parent", allowing them to get away with things that they shouldn't, and trying to be a friend to their child instead of a parent. An unstable home also includes a home where the parent or parents are busy doing their own thing, and the children are left unsupervised. In this case, life becomes total chaos and these kids end up raising themselves.

An example of a teen being raised in an unstable home is Holly Harvey, fifteen, from Georgia. Holly was initially raised by an unstable mother who was a single, drug-addicted stripper. When her mother was arrested and sent to jail, Holly moved in with her grandparents. Grandpa and Grandma laid down the rules of their home, which were not enforced at her mother's home. The rules included "no sneaking out in the middle of the night," "no using drugs" and most devastating, "We forbid you to date your girlfriend." Holly was dating a female classmate, sixteen-year old Sandy Ketchum. Holly and Sandy were in love, and they wanted to spend the rest of their lives together. But this arrangement didn't fit into Grandpa and Grandma's Baptist beliefs. As you will see in later chapters, the most dangerous trigger for female teen killers is when their parents, grandparents or legal guardian forbid them to date someone. Eventually, this led to the death of Holly's grandparents.

Holly was not going to stop her activity of sneaking out to see her girlfriend in the middle of the night, nor was she going to stop using drugs or dating Sandy. After her grandparents established their new household rules, she threatened to kill both of them within days, which is a major warning sign. She then grabbed two knives out the kitchen butcher block, took them downstairs to her bedroom, and practiced stabbing the mattress for a week as she prepared to make good on her threat to kill her grandparents. For this reason, I warn parents, grandparents and other adults about the dangers of bringing troubled teens and children into their homes, especially when they have their own children. Parkland, Florida school shooter Nikolas Cruz was a troubled teen, brought into a friend's family home. They are lucky they are all still alive today, as Cruz shot 34 people, killing 17 at his former school.

On August 2, 2004, Holly snuck her girlfriend Sandy into her grandparents' home, and they attacked, stabbing them both to death with large kitchen knives. As they stabbed Grandma to death, they yelled "Die Bitch!" They chased Grandpa throughout the house, finally catching him in the kitchen, slicing his throat and stabbing him to death. Grandpa tried to call the police during the attack, but he only succeeded in pulling the phone cord out of the wall. The two female teen killers fled in Grandpa's truck, along with money and jewelry, and headed to Tybee Island, Georgia. Law enforcement were able to locate them by tracking their cell phones and they were arrested the next morning. The teen killers were sentenced to twenty years in prison and are currently approaching their parole dates. Holly was arrested with a murder to-do list written on her arm that read "keys, kill, money, jewelry."

Clifford Davis, from Bradenton, Florida, suffered abuse as he was raised by his single mother. Along with being abused by his own mother, his father told him he was never wanted. On December 4, 2005, he decided to kill his abusive mother, Stephanie Davis, as well as his grandfather, Joel Hill. He strangled his mother to death in their apartment, and then proceeded to have sex with her corpse. He stole money from her and went shopping at the local mall. After returning from the mall, he lured his grandfather to his apartment, where he also killed him. His grandfather was strangled, stabbed, and killed as Davis duct taped his body and stood on his neck. Prosecutors stated that the motive was "hatred and greed," and defense attorneys claimed he was mentally ill and obsessed with violence, including violent video games. Relatives and family members said he suffered from abuse, isolation and depression. Davis smirked and smiled as the judge read him his punishment, life in prison with no parole.

CAUSE NUMBER THREE-BULLYING AT SCHOOL OR AT HOME

Bullying is the number three cause of teen murder, but the overwhelming number one cause of school shootings today. In my research, nearly every school shooter was bullied, mostly by classmates at school. From Luke Woodham to Barry Loukaitis, Kip Kinkel, Nikolas Cruz, and Andy Williams; it is a common thread.

Kip Kinkel was being bullied by a football player, and tired of the harassment. He even had a picture of the football team hanging in his locker, with his bully circled and the words "kill" written above his head. After being caught with a loaded gun in his locker, and being arrested and expelled, Kinkel went home and killed his parents. He returned to get even with his classmates and attempt to kill his bully. On May 21, 1998, Kinkel opened fire on Thurston High School in Springfield, Oregon, shooting 24 victims and killing two students. After killing his parents and two students at school, Kinkel's death toll ended at four. He was fascinated with guns, bombs and knives, having illegally purchased three stolen guns, collecting three dozen knives and had been building bombs in his home. Kinkel also suffered from mental illness and told the police that the voices in his head were telling him to kill. His final act of his mission was to kill as many students as he could, kill first responders from the roof of the school, then kill himself, but he was tackled by fellow students and was unable to complete that act. He was arrested, convicted of multiple murders, and sentenced to life in prison without parole.

Luke Woodham, 16, from Pearl, Mississippi, was another school shooter who was bullied mercilessly for nearly all of his school career. He was punched, kicked, spit on, and had urine thrown on him. Woodham also had his pants pulled down in the cafeteria, and it was reported that some teachers even took part in the harassment. After being rebuffed by a girl he liked, and tired of the abuse at home by his single mother, he made a decision to become a school shooter and set the date of October 1, 1997 as his target to end his pain.

Woodham, after killing his own dog and setting it on fire, killed his mother in their home using a knife and baseball bat. He then grabbed a loaded rifle, jumped into his mother's car and drove to Pearl High School. He entered the school yelling "This ends now!" and proceeded to walk up to the girl he liked, Christina, and shot her in the chest, killing her. Claiming that he didn't understand why he completed the next action, he shot and killed Christina's good friend Lydia. He then ran through the school shooting random students, seven in total, with none of the injuries being fatal. He explained that he was in a trance-like state, and "It was like I was there, but I wasn't..." After shooting the students he wanted to shoot, he exited the building. Woodham had trouble getting his mother's car started. Because of the vehicle malfunction, he was apprehended by an assistant principal with a gun, and his murderous rampage was stopped. Luke Woodham confessed, and reported that he felt remorse and explained why he carried out his murderous rampage. Ultimately, Woodham was convicted and sentence to three life sentences, which ensures he will never live outside of barbed wired encased prison walls.

CAUSE NUMBER FOUR-OBSESSION WITH VIOLENT ENTERTAINMENT

You can't discuss the rise of teen violence, teen murder and school massacres without giving an earnest look at the research that reflects the contribution of media violence to the paradigm of teen violence. Today, we are raising a generation with violent first-person shooter video games, torture films, violent music and violent pornography. The teen murder rate is staying consistent at around five teen murders per day, and our current decade is the deadliest in school shootings, with the highest numbers ever reported. Today's teens are violent, killing each other, or their classmates at alarming rates. You can't eliminate the violent culture our children and teens are immersed in today. Our current generation is encapsulated in a culture of death. There is a direct correlation in the increase in teen murders and school massacres subsequent to the release of violent first-person shooter video games and other violent teen entertainment.

Mainstream music today has declined with the advent of negative and violent messages in lyrics and videos, laced with gory obscenities, and spreading the drug, sex and violent culture to our most innocent ears and eyes. Some of the most violent rappers are even awarded as top artists throughout the music industry from year to year. Names like Eminem, 21 Savage, Rhianna, 2 Chains and Lil Wayne top the charts. Torture films have become a relentless normal staple of teen culture, with titles such as Saw, Evil Dead, Last House on the Left and Hostel playing at mainstream movie theaters. Video games have evolved from innocent games like Pac Man and Super Mario to violent games including (but certainly not limited to): Grand Theft Auto, Manhunt, Hatred, Halo and Modern Warfare. It's of no surprise that numerous teen killers and almost all school shooters are or were obsessed with violent entertainment, especially violent video games.

Danny Petric, obsessed with the Halo video game franchise, was inconsolable when his father took his latest purchase away from him, Halo's latest release. He retaliated by stealing his game back, along with a loaded handgun, and then shooting both of his parents as they napped in the living room. Danny played his violent video games non-stop when he wasn't at school. He later explained that the game controlled him. Petric was raised by an intact, church-going family headed by married parents, and by all appearances, was a healthy member of a normal, loving family. Danny's mother died due to his murderous actions, but his father miraculously survived a devastating point-blank gunshot to his head. Danny was convicted in the murder of his mother and is serving a lengthy prison sentence before he has a chance at parole.

Two other killers were obsessed with violent and depressing media, but on the outside appeared as two average teens while being raised in an upscale community by typical suburban parents. But something was brewing in Littleton, Colorado, and Dylan Klebold and Eric Harris were far from typical kids. On April 20, 1999, Harris and Klebold acted out their violent fantasies, many which were learned from the violent media they consumed. From the brutal video games, Doom and Duke Nukem, to the psychopathic serial killer movie, Natural Born Killers, these works served as models and inspiration for the young men's deadly actions. Harris and Klebold were obsessed with violence and reportedly wanted to carry out the biggest massacre in American and quite possibly, human history.

Planning their crime spree for eighteen months, and naming their massacre NBK after their favorite movie, Oliver Stone's Natural Born Killers, they had plans to blow up their high school and kill 500 students and teachers. They then planned to shoot the students who didn't die at the hands of their bombs. They also planned to drive to the Denver International Airport, hijack an airplane and then crash it into an unspecified location in New York City. Along with being fans of violent video games and movies, they also idolized Oklahoma City bomber Timothy McVeigh, and German dictator Adolph Hitler. I'm sure they were confident they would break McVeigh's mass murder record of 168 and become the deadliest mass murderers in American history. They also wanted to be famous and were hoping Oliver Stone would make a movie about them and tell their life stories.

Fortunately for the students at Columbine High School, they didn't kill 500, as their plans didn't pan out as they thought, and only killed 13. Thirteen deaths were the highest number for high school shooting deaths (by currently enrolled students as the perpetrators) for nearly twenty years until Parkland, Florida, where 17 students and staff members died. The Parkland shooter was not a currently enrolled student at the time of his massacre, but could have been. Klebold and Harris, making history as one of the most heinous and horrific school shooter duos, remain inspirational to numerous murderous teens who want to make a mark and go out in a blaze of glory.

Harris and Klebold were textbook school shooters, with numerous causes and warning signs. The causes included bullying, an obsession with multiple forms of violence, suicidal ideologies, obsession with violent entertainment, guns, bombs and knives, a possible cult obsession, Nazism, peer pressure, and a reported lack of spiritual guidance and discipline. The warning signs were multiferious, including threats of violence, violent postings, drawings, shooting of guns, obsession with violent movies and video games, and even a practice walk-through at the school with fake guns being allowed on campus under the guise of a school film project.

Other teen killers who were obsessed with violent media include Brian Draper, Tory Adamcik, Josh Phillips, and Richard Henderson. Draper and Adamcik were obsessed with horror movies and became thrill killers in Idaho. They wrote and filmed their own horror movie and enacted the crime with the real-life thrill killing of one of their female classmates. On September 22, 2006, Draper and Adamcik, wielding knives while donning masks, attacked their classmate Cassie as she was house sitting for her aunt and uncle. They stabbed her over twenty times and filmed themselves driving to and from the crime scene. They even filmed the victim at school the morning they killed her, asking her to say hello to the camera.

Jacksonville, Florida's Josh Phillips was given a computer in his bedroom with access to the Internet, and quickly became addicted to porn. Regular porn became boring and led to a progression to violent porn. For Josh, pornography wasn't enough, and he then moved to the next step…. He wanted to experience violent porn in real life, so he targeted a neighbor girl, Maddie. On November 3, 1998, Josh lured Maddie to his backyard, played a game with her, then dragged her into his home. He sexually assaulted her, beat her with a baseball bat, and then stabbed her five times in the neck, killing her. He hid her dead body under his waterbed, where her body remained for one week. Josh would go to school, help look for Maddie with the search crew, and literally sleep on top of her at night. One day his mother saw something leaking from under the bed, pulled the bed frame apart, and found little Maddie's body. Phillips was arrested, convicted, and sentenced to life in prison without parole.

Richard Henderson, 19, lived the good life in Bradenton, Florida with his family, within minutes of the beautiful beaches on the Gulf of Mexico. On Thursday, November 24, 2005, Thanksgiving Day, he was playing a video game with his eleven-year-old brother Jacob in a bedroom. Suddenly and for no reason, he pulled out a steel pipe and smashed his brother's head in, ending his brother's life in the bedroom. He tossed his dead body out the window of his mobile home bedroom. He continued to kill the rest of his family, beating them all to death with a steel pipe. Henderson killed his mother, his father, and his 82-year-old grandmother, beating them all to death in the head with the same steel pipe he killed his brother with. He then retrieved his brother's body from the yard and dragged him into the laundry room, where police found him. Henderson left a note on the bathroom sink confessing that he killed all his family and that he wanted to die for his crime. He explained in the note "I know I did it, but I don't know why. I did not kill them out of hate or selfishness…I'm so sorry mom, dad, grandma, bro. I deserve to die one billion times for each one of you. I felt useless." The note was signed "Richard." Richard was a Juggalo, a fan of the violent rap group Insane Clown Posse, or ICP. There have been thousands of crimes attributed to the fans of this group, including rape, murder, assault, kidnapping, and robberies. There have been so many crimes attributed to this group that the FBI has classified the fans as a hybrid gang.

CAUSE NUMBER FIVE-OBSESSION WITH DEADLY WEAPONS

Many teen killers and school shooters are obsessed with deadly weapons, including guns, knives, swords, hatchets, and explosives. Believe it or not, this is a positive because it is one of the ways we are able to catch and stop potential killers before they strike. Teens obsessed with deadly weapons love to do research, sketch, and talk about them, as well as post pictures of them on social media. An obsession with deadly weapons is both a cause and a warning sign, and should be taken seriously, especially if it is combined with threats of violence. Most school shooters were obsessed with guns, bombs and knives, including

Eric Harris, Dylon Klebold, Nikolas Cruz, Virginia Tech's Seung-Hui Cho, Sandy Hook's Adam Lanza, and the Jonesboro Killers.

As far as stopping teen killers from obtaining guns, there is a lot of talk about tightening up gun laws from the media and some politicians. When you study these killers like I do, you realize that tougher gun laws will not stop them. They obtain their guns from their own home or a relative's home, or obtain them illegally, including stealing or purchasing stolen guns. 80%, the majority of mass murderers, use handguns and approximately 10% use shotguns. The remaining offenders use various rifles. The least common rifle used is the AR-15. This gun has gained popularity due to its glorification in teen entertainment which includes violent video games such as Grand Theft Auto, as well as movies like Planet of the Apes and The Purge.

CAUSE NUMBER SIX-SUICIDAL IDEOLOGIES

There is a segment of teen killers who want to end their killing spree with suicide, by killing themselves. These kids are driven by anger, retaliation, fame, and suicidal fantasies. David Abrahamsen explained it brilliantly, and I have been seeing this description in my three decades of study and research.

"Every homicide is unconsciously a suicide, and every suicide is, in a sense, a psychological homicide. Typically, the killer is afraid of killing himself (or herself), afraid of dying, and therefore he (she) murders someone else." –David Abrahamsen, author of "The Murdering Mind."

The mass murderer and school shooter often have a suicide fantasy, and many of them end their mass killing with the killing of themselves. Killers who carried out mass shootings, and ended their own lives include: Virginia Tech, Sandy Hook, Las Vegas, Great Mills, Maryland, and Columbine. Many others desired to kill themselves according to interviews and reports after their arrests, but failed to accomplish their plan, such as the killers from Parkland, Florida and Springfield, Oregon.

Suicide has become a serious problem among our youth. According to a 2015 CDC report, the suicide rate for 15-19 year old females hit a forty year high in 2015. From 2007 to 2015, an eight year span, suicide rates for females doubled and suicide rates for males rose 30%. From 1975 to 2015, a forty year period, approximately 100,000 teens took their own lives.

Concerning suicide, the two biggest risk factors are past attempts (nearly half of all teens who complete a suicide tried unsuccessfully before) and a family history of suicide. The top warning sign for suicide is a threat of taking one's own life, such as "I should just kill myself" or "Nobody would miss me if I was gone." Another prime warning sign is a teen giving away prized possessions, which is typical behavior of one who is planning to end his or her life. Self-abuse is yet another warning sign of suicide, and many teen killers, school shooters and those who commit suicide begin their destructive behavior by harming themselves. This is done either by burning or cutting themselves. Females attempt suicide more, but males are more successful. Guns are used in approximately half of teen suicides, and the other half consists of various means, including hanging and drug overdose. Suicide is not more prevalent during the Christmas season, as some might believe. That is a myth, and experts report that the highest months of teen suicide are the summer months of April, May, June and July. For help with suicidal teens, visit AFSP.org, Suicidology.org, and JasonFoundation.com. You can also call 1-800-SUICIDE.

CAUSE NUMBER SEVEN-USE OF ILLEGAL DRUGS, ALCOHOL AND MEDICATION

Many teen killers and school shooters are intoxicated when they kill by using alcohol, illegal drugs, and/or prescription medication. School killer Nikolas Cruz, family killer Blaine Ross, and thrill killer Craig Price all used drugs prior to their murderous actions. Parkland, Florida school killer Cruz talked about using various drugs, including prescription medication and marijuana.

Blaine Ross killed his parents while they slept in their Bradenton, Florida home on January 7, 2004, with his motive being financial gain.

He killed his parents, Richard and Kathleen Ross with a baseball bat while high on cocaine and Xanax. He was sentenced to death in 2007 but has since been resentenced to life without parole. His statement at the trial was "I would first like to apologize to my family. I have taken something very dear from you and I know this. I don't know what happened. I'm am sorry. There are more people involved including Michael Young. He killed my Mom. I killed my Dad. It's not an excuse, but I was high on cocaine and Xanax. But I didn't man up and stop it."

Craig Price, known as "The Warwick Slasher," is the youngest modern-day serial killer, actually being the youngest since 14-year-old Jesse Pomeroy in 1872. Pomeroy killed two little boys and tortured several others. Price killed four victims by the age of 15 and began killing at the age of thirteen, a year younger than Pomeroy. He struck fear in his neighborhood in Warwick, Rhode Island, killing one victim at the age of thirteen, and three more victims at the age of fifteen. He was arrested in 1989 for four murders, with the only criminal history he had prior to this crime as petty theft.

On July 27, 1987, Price killed a 27-year-old female two houses away from his, stabbing her 58 times with a knife from her own kitchen. Two years later, on September 1, 1989, he broke into the home of another neighbor and murdered three female victims while high on marijuana and LSD. He killed a 39-year-old mother, stabbing her 57 times. He also killed her 10-year-old daughter, stabbing her 57 times and killed her 8 year- old daughter, stabbing her 30 times and smashing her skull. Some feel the motive of the murders were anger and hate, as Price had experienced discrimination due to his race, as a child. It is reported that he may have been "paying back" white society for the injustice he felt they imposed upon him in his formative years.

Price confessed to four murders with little emotion, and because of his age and the laws in his state, he was sentenced as a minor, to be locked up until his 21st birthday. His crimes culminated with a 5-year sentence for four homicides. He bragged that he would "make history" when he was released, which was a big mistake on his part. The public rallied for Price to be incarcerated longer than he was sentenced to, and luckily for those who opposed his release, Price did not stay out of trouble in prison.

Due to his behavior and crimes in prison, Price was sentenced to an additional 10-25 years depending on his behavior. Price was moved to a Florida prison, and has continued to be a problem for the Florida Department of Corrections. He was eligible for parole in 2009 but was denied release. He was again eligible for parole in 2020, but on April 4, 2017, Price was accused of stabbing a fellow inmate, Joshua Davis, at the Suwannee Correctional Institution in Live Oak, Florida with a 5-inch homemade knife. He may have been given additional time for that offense.

CAUSE NUMBER EIGHT-THE THIRST FOR FAME

This cause is something I have added to my list since the release of my first book, "Inside the Mind of a Teen Killer." I have noticed as the American news media makes teen killers and school shooters famous, more and more are attracted to the prospect of becoming a celebrity. School killer Nikolas Cruz bragged in a video prior to his school shooting that he would be famous, and everyone would know his name. He even named several networks that would talk about him. And his prediction came true, as CNN, FoxNews, MSNBC, USA Today and others broadcasted his name non-stop for days, giving him the fame he craved. And as they make killers famous, they are putting out a casting call for the next mass killer, school shooter, or teen killer.

Luke Woodham, the Pearl, Mississippi school killer also knew that fame for his crimes would come. After Woodham killed his mother and two classmates, and subsequently shot and injured seven more classmates, he stated in his post-murder spree interview with police, "I guess I'm going to be pretty famous." And famous he became. School killers and mass murderers have graced the covers of numerous magazines and newspapers, including the Columbine killers on the cover of Time Magazine, the Boston Marathon bomber on the cover of Rolling Stone Magazine, the Jonesboro, Arkansas killers also on the cover of Time magazine, and Luke Woodham, the Pearl, Mississippi school killer on the cover of People Magazine.

It seems that the mainstream media can't wait to broadcast the killer's name and face, giving him or her instant fame. Imagine how much you would have to spend to get a national news media outlet to run a commercial about you for several hours a day, and possibly all week long. How many millions would you pay for such publicity? That is exactly what the mainstream media gives every mass murderer, school killer and mass shooter. In Canada, they don't have a custom of releasing the name, picture or identity of a juvenile killer, guaranteeing that nobody outside of the town or school where the event happened will know who the killer is. It is time for American mainstream media outlets to stop mentioning the killers' names, stop plastering their pictures all over their news reports, and stop giving them the fame they crave. As networks like CNN, FoxNews and MSNBC blame the President, the NRA, guns, mental illness and violent entertainment, maybe they should be introspective and realize that they are a vital part of the problem and not of the solution.

CAUSE NUMBER NINE-CULTS, GANGS AND HATE GROUPS

Cults, gangs and hate groups have always been a cause of teen murder. Gangs include the mainstream gangs like the Bloods, the Crips, MS-13 and more. They can also be more localized gangs, which are specific to one city. Cults include Satanists, Juggalos, and hate groups like the Black Panthers, the KKK, and white supremacy. Nathan Brooks was an Ohio teen killer who murdered his parents in Bellaire, Ohio. He turned from being an altar boy to becoming a Satanist. He felt by killing people he would please Satan, so he assembled a hit list of 13 people and set out to kill all thirteen. In the end, he killed his mother and father, stabbing his mother to death in her bed, and then shooting and killing his father in his bed. He later beheaded his father and used his head in a Satanic ritualistic ceremony. The members of these groups are dedicated to their cause and are willing to carry out various crimes, including violent crimes like assault, rape, robbery, and murder.

CAUSE NUMBER TEN-PEER PRESSURE

Believe or not, teens are easily influenced by their friends to do crazy things, whether it be vandalism, petty crimes or more serious, life threatening acts. Peer pressure does play a role in teen murder. Many teen killers are arrested as a group or a duo, with one teen influencing and peer pressuring the others. At Columbine, Dylan Klebold was ultimately pressured by his close friend, Eric Harris. Because of the social dynamic between the two, Harris inspired and influenced Klebold. Eric Harris was the true leader and the real psychopath behind the Columbine mass murder.

In Madison, Indiana, when one girl wanted twelve-year-old Shanda Sharer dead, she recruited three friends to help her torture and murder the innocent young victim. On January 10, 1992, Melinda Loveless, 14, jealous about a girl Shanda was dating, recruited Toni Lawrence, 15, Hope Rippey, 15, and Laurie Tackett, 17, to help kill Shanda Sharer. Loveless showed the girls a knife she had-the knife she planned to scare Shanda with, because she felt Shanda stole her girlfriend away from her. In the course of the night, the four girls picked up Shanda, abducted her, tied her up with rope, beat her, stripped her naked, stabbed her, and then set her on fire. They placed her body in the trunk and beat her with a tire iron. Eventually they took her out of the trunk, set her on fire and burned her alive. Three of the four girls have already been released from prison, and Loveless will be released as well.

A similar crime occurred near Morgantown, West Virginia on July 6, 2012, when sixteen-year-old Skylar Neese disappeared from her Star City, West Virginia home. Her body was found nine days later in Pennsylvania, and to the shock of everyone, her two good friends Sheila Eddy, 17, and Rachel Shoaf, 16, were arrested for her murder. On the night of her murder, Skylar snuck out of her home around midnight, and joined Eddy and Shoaf, unaware of their murderous plans. With kitchen knives taken from their homes, Shoaf and Eddy stabbed Neese to death as she fought for her life. The young girl was stabbed nearly 50 times before they dumped her body near the side of the road. On March 13, after a long investigation, and thanks to an anonymous tip, Shanda's body was recovered, and Eddy and Shoaf were arrested. They both confessed, took plea deals, and have a chance for parole in ten to fifteen years.

On January 27, 2001, in Etna, New Hampshire, Robert Tulloch, 17, and James Parker, 16, were arrested for the "Dartmouth Murders," a brutal slaying of Half and Susanne Zantop, both professors at Dartmouth College. Tulloch, president of his class, was the leader of this murderous act and his schoolmate, Parker, active in the school drama club, was Tulloch's follower. Together, they planned to kill numerous people, and rob their victims to amass a fortune. Initially, they planned the murder of an entire family, chose a nice home with a BMW in the driveway and showed up at 10pm at night. Luckily for the homeowner, he had a gun, and chased them off with it.

Feeling that they failed because it was late at night, they chose a remote home and approached the home on a Saturday afternoon, during daylight hours. Holding clipboards and pens, they knocked on the door and explained they were doing a survey for school on the environment. The couple let them in, and within minutes, Tulloch and Parker stabbed the couple to death, and sliced their throats. They took some money and fled, but were arrested shortly thereafter by the police tracing a knife sheath they dropped at the crime scene. The knife sheath was unique and was easily traced back to the home of the murderous teens. At trial, Parker pled guilty and testified against Tulloch. He received a twenty-five-year sentence, allowing him the chance for parole after sixteen years. Tulloch was convicted of first degree murder and sentenced to life without parole. Tulloch was the leader of the two, and demanded that James Parker stab Mrs. Zantop to death, which he did.

CAUSE NUMBER ELEVEN-POVERTY AND FASCINATION WITH CRIME

Poverty and the criminal lifestyle go hand-in-hand and can lead to teen murder. In large urban areas like Chicago and Houston, we have high homicide rates. There is a mixture of gangs, narcotic sales, violent crime and prostitution that leads to high homicide rates. But at the foundation of all these crimes is poverty. Poverty is the number one contributor to urban homicide. Like I always tell my live audiences, I am not saying if you are poor you are going to become a killer, but it is definitely a part of the puzzle. I don't meet too many rich kids in prison, as our prisons and death rows are filled with poor people.

CAUSE NUMBER TWELVE-NO SPIRITUAL GUIDANCE AND NO DISCIPLINE

Through my formative years in elementary school in Cleveland and later in middle school in Aurora, Ohio, I experienced discipline at school. When I acted up at Holy Name Elementary School, the nuns let me know if I was "acting a fool", and disciplined me. Their discipline methods usually rotated with each infraction as a hair pull, an ear pull, or a whack of a ruler across my knuckles. At Harmon Middle School in Aurora, Ohio, I was given a swat with a paddle by one of the principals. That swat hurt me physically and corrected my behavior. I made sure to never do again what I did to get into trouble. I would also be disciplined by my parents at home, which helped to curb my bad behavior.

Fast forward to today with some forms of school discipline now illegal, and home discipline quickly becoming archaic, we see bad behavior by teens going unpunished. My wife, who is a middle school teacher, will tell me stories about her students who will confront her in the classroom, yelling "fuck you" or asking her "why do you have to be a bitch?" Why do they display these behaviors? Because there are no consequences, no negative repercussions. Yes, they get a card signed, and yes, they can get in-school or out-of-school suspension. But with parents who would rather turn their cheek to their child's bad behavior and be their friends, there are usually no consequences at all.

CAUSE NUMBER THIRTEEN-MENTAL ILLNESS

My last cause on my thirteen causes list is mental illness, which includes brain injuries. When some try to explain why teens kill, and they don't understand all the pieces of the puzzle, they simply blame it on mental illness. Because, surely, those who take other people's lives must be crazy. Believe or not, they don't have to be insane. Of course, it depends on what your definition is of mental illness. Some mental illness definitions include depression or narcissism as mental illness. But in my professional opinion, as someone who has interviewed and researched hundreds upon hundreds of cases, mental illness is the courtroom definition, which means the killer didn't understand his or her actions, and they didn't know what they were doing. Using that definition, most killers are not mentally ill. And that includes serial killers, mass murderers, school shooters and teen killers.

I talk to real life monsters, real boogeymen, and as heinous as their crimes are, most are not mentally ill. Most know exactly what they are doing, know their actions are wrong, and do their best not to get caught. In saying that, there are approximately 10 to 20 percent of teen killers who are mentally ill, bi-polar, schizophrenic, and/or maniac depressive. Some are truly mentally ill and hear voices. School killers Kipland Kinkel from Springfield, Oregon and Nikolas Cruz from Parkland, Florida both reported hearing voices in their heads. There are some who do experience this, and unfortunately, there is little treatment for them today. Up until the mid-1960's, there were a significant number of psychiatric hospitals throughout the United States. But today, most have been closed and treatment for the mentally ill is scarce and expensive. Most of our mentally ill are homeless or are in prison. Much of our mental health care now has been shifted to correctional facilities. There are many debates about the deinstitutionalization of psychiatric hospitals that has led to the current mental health crisis we are experiencing today. And to those who always blame mental illness, this is an insult to those who struggle with mental illness, as most mentally ill people are not violent and do not commit murder. Only 3-5% of mentally ill people are violent.

CHAPTER THREE
THE WARNING SIGNS OF TEEN KILLERS AND SCHOOL SHOOTERS

1-CRUELTY TO ANIMALS

This is the single most dangerous warning sign of a possible teen killer, school shooter, mass murderer and a future serial killer. This warning sign is part of the Homicidal Triad, also known as the Macdonald Triad. Teen killers and school shooters will experiment with the killing and torture of animals, acting out their young fantasies. Serial killers will experiment with killing animals, then graduate to killing humans, usually mimicking the method in which they killed animals.

Jeffrey Dahmer picked up a dead dog and cut the head off, displaying it in his yard. He would later kill men, remove their heads, and keep them in his refrigerator. Dennis Rader, BTK, which stands for "Bind, Torture, Kill," would bind and torture cats and strangle them with a cord. Then he would hang them inside a barn. This is a very ominous warning sign for a child to display. Later in life, he would bind and torture real people, strangling them with a cord and his bare hands. Among his many murders, he eventually hung an eleven-year-old female, Josephine Otero, from a basement water pipe in 1974.

Steven Avery, of the notorious Netflix show "Making a Murderer," was convicted of killing a female photographer and burning her body in a bonfire, and then a burn barrel. As a teen, he allegedly would burn cats alive in burn barrels and bonfires. As you see, psychopaths will experiment with homicide on animals, and if they enjoy the act, will graduate to humans. Many teen killers and school shooters participated in animal cruelty and the killing of animals as well. Luke Woodham, the Pearl, Mississippi school shooter, before his murderous rampage, was beating his dog on a regular basis. When his mom noticed the dog was limping and was going to take it to the veterinarian, Luke told his mother that the dog ran away. He then took the dog out into the woods and poured kerosene on the dog and into its mouth. Woodham set the dog on fire and threw the burning animal into a pond.

Parkland, Florida school shooter Nikolas Cruz told investigators that he killed animals growing up, including shooting birds and squirrels.

If you know of a juvenile who is killing or torturing animals, this is a serious warning sign and predictor of future violence. Take the necessary steps to protect the public and report this behavior.

2-THREATS OF MURDER

Normal talk in your home from your teen might be "I hate this family" or "I hate you," but threats of "I'm going to kill you" or "I'm going to kill this whole family" should be taken seriously. Making a statement or threat about killing or harming someone is a serious threat and one of the top warning signs. And if the threat is against a specific person, it is even more dangerous. Nikolas Cruz bragged on a social media post that he was going to be "a professional school shooter," and in a video he posted, he talked about killing his classmates and boasted that everyone will know who he is very soon. On August 16, 2011, Jared Cano, from Tampa, Florida, bragged in a video how he was going to be the next famous Tampa, Florida school shooter, even detailing his plans of bombing his school and shooting his fellow students. He posted his video to social media, and luckily someone saw it and reported it. He was arrested, convicted, and sentenced to twenty years in a state prison.

3-FASCINATION WITH FIRE

This is another dangerous warning sign and is part of the Homicidal Triad, also known as the Macdonald Triad. Setting things on fire, like storage sheds or bedroom carpet is a hallmark of future violence. This also includes an interest in explosives and bombs. If you remember Luke Woodham, not only did he kill his family pet, but the method of killing it was fire, burning his dog alive. Nikolas Cruz also bragged about playing with fire near his home. Many serial killers were fascinated with fire, including David "Son of Sam" Berkowitz, who set over 1000 fires and watched the police and fire departments respond. Setting fires allows the pyromaniac the chance to control the police, the fire department, and cause fear among the citizens in their community.

4-MAJOR INCIDENT AT SCOOL OR HOME

An embarrassing incident at school for a troubled student can result in a deadly scenario. There is nothing as dangerous as being bullied or embarrassed at school that has the potential to drive today's teens to violence. Moses Lake school shooter Barry Loukaitis told me about an incident that occurred at his school prior to his attack. Barry explained that he was in his eighth-grade art class when some girls were making fun of him, the way he looked and the way he dressed. In the midst of this bullying incident, Barry's bully walked into class and decided to join in as well, calling Barry a "faggot" in front of the whole class. Barry told me that at that moment, he knew he would kill Manual Vela. On February 2, 1996, he came through on his promise. He opened fire on his Algebra class, shooting four and killing three. Among the dead were his bully and his teacher. He explained to me that the abusive incident in art class was the last provocation and ultimately led to his decision to murder.

In Santa Fe, Texas on May 18, 2018, Dimitrios Pagourtzis, 17, opened fire at his school killing eight students and two teachers, and injuring thirteen others. He used a shotgun and .38 revolver owned by his father. In my research and interviews, this is typically how school shooters obtain their weapons. The killer wore a trench coat daily, and he had numerous plans recorded in a journal and on his cell phone. The shooting occurred shortly after classes began. Another important piece of my research is that the first hour of school is the deadliest hour. Explosive devices were found near the school. The incident lasted twenty five minutes, until police could wound the suspect and Pagourtzis then surrendered.

Even though he was on the honor roll and football team, many claim he was the victim of bullying, by students and possibly coaches. He had posted a picture of himself on social media the day before wearing a shirt that read "born to kill." It was reported that a female called out the shooter during class prior to the shooting, telling him that she was not interested in dating him, which embarrassed him and possibly acted as a trigger.

5-BEDWETTING INTO TEEN YEARS

Bedwetting, also called enuresis, is not only a sign of possible trauma and abuse, but can be a warning sign and predictor of future suicide and violence. A reason why this is a predictor is because this act is an emotional behavior, which could be tied to psychological problems. Studies have also linked enuresis to genetics, hormones, and as prevalent in combination with ADHD. For a small percent of children, it is at most times uncontrollable and nocturnal enuresis lasts well beyond the scope of what is considered normal. On the other side, enuresis can also be a physical ailment that can be treated by the medical community. Either way, a child with this problem should definitely be taken to seek medical attention. There are some who don't feel bedwetting is a warning sign of violence, but in my research, it is not only prevalent, but significant.

6-PEEPING TOM & VOYEURISM

I have included this indicator as an addition to the "homicidal triad," which makes it no longer a "triad", but I feel it is one of the predictors of future serial killers and teen killers. This act usually begins with what some feel is just harmless peeping, which I strongly disagree with. In my personal opinion, I don't see anything harmless about being a voyeur. After one gets comfortable with peeping, the next step is a bit bolder. Many budding teen killers and serial killers will actually enter the home when it is unoccupied and steal women's undergarments. I feel this is practice for the next and final step, entering homes to rape and murder its occupants, usually women.

Edward O'Brien, 15, from Somerville, Massachusetts was peeping on his best friend's mother, 42, through her living room windows while hiding in the bushes for months. It was also reported that he was spying on her from across the street where he lived, using a telescope. One day in 1995 he caught Janet Downing sleeping on the couch, snuck into her home, and murdered her. He stabbed her 98 times, and her body was found by her son on the dining room floor. O'Brien was 6 foot 6, weighed 270, and was arrested with cuts on his arms and hands.

It was debated whether O'Brien had sex with Downing's corpse. Ironically, he served communion at church the following Sunday as an altar boy. He claimed he was innocent, but blood and fingerprint evidence at the scene proved otherwise. O' Brien was sentenced to life in prison at age 15, but due to his age at the time of the murder, he is now eligible for parole after serving 15 years of his life sentence.

Many sex killers and rapists begin their sex crimes with voyeuristic activities, usually peeping at first, and following the pattern like I discussed above. These perpetrators eventually get bolder and enter homes, steal personal undergarments and then go back to commit murders. Harvey Robinson and Dennis Rader both started as teenagers when committing these acts and continued on to become serial killers.

7-THREATS OF SUICIDE

Suicidal thoughts and ideations are warning signs of possible future violence. David Abrahamsen, the author of "The Murdering Mind" stated, "Every homicide is unconsciously a suicide, and every suicide is, in a sense, a psychological homicide. Typically, the killer is afraid of killing himself, afraid of dying, and therefore, he or she murders someone else." Suicide has increased during the last ten years among our youth, and this suicidal act can very easily lead to a homicidal act. Some just want to kill themselves, and some want to take others with them. Adults will do the same thing. Along with approximately five teen killers every day, we have the following stats about the increase of teen suicide during the last ten years, from research conducted by the CDC, or The Centers for Disease Control. According to the CDC, in a study conducted in 2015, the last year they conducted this research, they found that suicide doubled among teen girls from 2007 to 2015 and rose 30% during the same time period for teen boys. The two biggest contributing factors leading to completed teen suicides include past suicide attempts (nearly half of teens who kill themselves have attempted once before) and a family history of suicide. Suicide is the third leading cause of death for 15-24-year old adolescents and young adults, according to the CDC, after accidents and homicides. More female teens attempt suicide, but more male teens complete the act. Contrary to popular belief, suicides are not more prevalent during the Christmas season for teens. In fact, the top suicide months for teens are April, May, June and July. Bullying is a major cause of teen suicide, as well as breakups with boyfriends and girlfriends. The top warning signs of teen suicide include a threat of suicide, giving away one's prized possessions, and a solid plan on how he or she wants to end his or her life. Any threat about suicide should be taken seriously, and the person making the threat should be given psychiatric help as soon as possible. There are several resources for help with suicidal family members, including AFSP.org, Suicidology.org, JasonFoundation.com, as well as the help hotlines 1-800- SUICIDE and 1-800-273-8255.

8-LEAKAGE OF VIOLENT THOUGHTS & FANTASIES

This warning sign is obvious, and can be seen in violent schoolwork, violent artwork, dark poetry, troubling posts on social media, and in personal journals. Sometimes this is a cry for help, and other times it is a true plan for future violence and mayhem. All threats should be taken seriously, even when the juvenile insists he or she is joking. Would you joke with an airport security worker about a bomb in your suitcase? The same punishment should result when a student jokes about murder and school violence. Teens with violent thoughts, fantasies and murderous plans have trouble keeping them inside, and usually tell someone or post something online. I call this "leakage," where the violence cannot be contained, and leaks out.

9-FASCINATION WITH GUNS, BOMBS AND KNIVES

Teens who post pictures on Facebook, Instagram, Snapchat, YouTube and Twitter of holding a weapon, like a gun or a knife, is a very dangerous warning sign. Teen killers and school shooters are fascinated with guns, knives, swords, hatchets, bombs and other dangerous weapons. Many school shooters illegally acquire guns, collect knives and build explosive devices. This is a nonnegotiable, and when you see this warning sign, an action should be taken immediately. Nikolas Cruz posted pictures of himself holding guns and knives on social media prior to the Parkland, Florida massacre. The 2017 Sutherland, Texas church shooter posted a picture of his rifle on social media, with the description "she's a bad bitch." The Columbine killers made videos of themselves shooting guns, and the Virginia Tech killer took photos of himself holding two handguns, the same two handguns he used in the Virginia Tech massacre.

10-OBSESSION WITH VIOLENT ENTERTAINMENT

We will cover this topic more in chapter five, but teens who are obsessed with violent video games, violent torture films, violent music and violent porn are more prone to violence than those who enjoy healthier forms of entertainment. It could be that these violent vehicles propel them to actual violence, or that violent teens gravitate to violent media because they have an interest in violence. Either way, in my opinion, it is a deadly combination, and is equivalent to pouring gasoline on a fire.

Those who consume violence take offense to my concern with an obsession with violent entertainment and don't fully understand my reason for including this warning sign. I explain it like this, "I don't think if you play violent video games you are going to kill people, since millions of teens play those games. But if you kill people, you can be sure that you play violent video games." I have never interviewed a teen killer or school shooter who killed someone and said that his favorite artist was Carrie Underwood. That has never occurred in my research. I'm being factious, but I think the point is obvious. Teen killers and school shooters love violent media, and in my opinion, it does affect them, and contributes to their violent ideologies and homicidal fantasies.

Teen killer Devin Thompson was obsessed with the cop-killing video game Grand Theft Auto, and he killed an entire law enforcement staff in a police station in Alabama, and then stole a police car, just like he did in his favorite game. Danny Petric loved first person shooter games like Halo, and when his parents took his game from him, he opened fire on them in their Ohio living room, killing his mother and seriously injuring his father. The Columbine killers loved their favorite movie so much that they watched it fifty times, and went so far as naming their shooting NBK, after their favorite movie, Natural Born Killers.

11-JOURNAL, BLOG OR SOCIAL MEDIA PAGE OF VIOLENT PLANS AND THOUGHTS

When we suspect a juvenile is considering a violent act, be it suicide or homicide, I encourage parents and professionals to look for a place where teens might record their thoughts and fantasies. This could be a journal, a blog, or a social media page. Alyssa Bustamante journaled her thoughts for months before carrying out her murder. She would write in a written journal about her desire to commit murder, and her need to experience what it feels like to kill someone. After killing her young female neighbor, she journaled her confession and described how she killed her. The Columbine killers had pages and pages of journals that they called their "manifesto." Nikolas Cruz liked to post on social media, in which he said he was going to be a "professional school shooter." He also posted videos detailing his plans, how he was going to do it, and that he not only would become famous, but would probably not survive.

Jared Cano, 18, from Tampa, Florida kept a journal of his plans to attack Freedom High School in April of 2011, and made a video detailing his plans. His plans were to detonate bombs and shoot innocent students. His video included lines like "The bombs blow at 7:26, then I'm going to advance on the courtyard." He described shooting several innocent students, multiple staff members, but making sure one staff member survived. Thankfully, someone was watching, and reported him. Before he could carry out his attack, he was arrested and sentenced to 20 years in a Florida state prison.

12-FASCINATION WITH MASS MURDER AND OTHER VIOLENT CRIMES

Teens who are planning a murder or a school shooting are usually studying other killers' works. It is not uncommon for school shooters to be fans of Dylan Klebold and Eric Harris. Many teen killers study other crimes and murders, learning important crime details that they aspire to carry out in their crimes. Many school shooters study other school shooters and learn from their mistakes, as well as copy and emulate what went right. Most try to improve on what went wrong with an earlier predecessor, hoping that their crime will be much more deadly, and much more shocking. Unfortunately, the mainstream media plays right into this, giving these killers celebrity status and inspiring the next wave of teen killers, school shooters and mass murderers.

13-FASCINATION WITH VIOLENT IDEOLOGIES

Teens who begin to follow violent or dark ideologies, like Satanism, White Supremacy or street gangs like Bloods, Crips and MS-13 may be headed down the road towards homicide. Be aware and look for books and pamphlets, or social media sites and webpages that they may frequent or follow that promote violent and dark beliefs. Cults and hate groups inspire up and coming killers and give them a cause and a reason to kill. Watch for change in behavior, clothing and friends.

In 1995, 17-year-old Nathan Brooks from St. Clairsville, Ohio wanted to please Satan, so breaking all Ten Commandments was the motivating factor for his crimes. One of the Ten Commandments, "thou shalt not murder" was the final commandment he broke, killing his parents and then decapitating his father's head with a hacksaw for a Satanic ritual. Many gang members have killed others when disrespected, and many cult members like the Juggalos have killed after being inspired by their group.

14-PARTICIPATION IN LESSER CRIMES

Some teen killers and school shooters will begin their life of crime with vandalism, shoplifting, assault or sexual crimes. This may be just typical teenage shenanigans, or it could be a future predictor of heinous and serious crimes. Many teen killers and school shooters have a history of petty crimes, like the Columbine killers. But just as many have no history of crime, which is why this warning sign is near the bottom.

15-CUTTING AND SELF-HARM

Many teen killers, school shooters and those who committed suicide began by harming themselves, usually by cutting or burning. Self-injury isn't always a sign of homicide, but it is a cry for help, and can be a sign of possible suicide. A 2018 study by the National Alliance on Mental Illness reported that teens and young adults diagnosed with a "self-harm" injury had nearly 27 times higher risk of suicide in the next year than peers who didn't self-harm. Self mutilation is common among young people today and could just be a way to release pain. Although many may not understand, self-injury is addictive, like pornography, and can be hard to overcome. When you discover a child is partaking in self-injury behavior, he or she should be provided an opportunity to speak to a licensed mental health professional, in the event that suicide, or homicide are possible intentions. Juveniles will cut or burn their arms, legs, or other body parts. They also can harm themselves by removing scabs, or by snapping themselves with a rubber band on their wrist. You can seek help and get more understanding at selfinjury.com and twloha.com.

CHAPTER FOUR
THE TRIGGERS THAT CAUSE TEENS TO KILL

In review, it takes three to six of my causes to create a teen killer. Many school shooters have as many as eight causes of teen murder. When it comes to warning signs, really, it only takes one sign to cause concern. But every teen killer and school shooter need a trigger, someone or something to push them toward homicide. It takes a trigger to make a normal teen become a killer.

Remember, it only takes one trigger, and triggers should be taken very seriously. Here are the six triggers that cause normal teens to become killers and school shooters.

1-DUMPED BY A GIRLFRIEND OR BOYFRIEND

This trigger is the number one trigger for male teen killers and male school shooters. According to my research, bullying is the leading cause of school shootings, but being rebuffed by a female is the leading trigger for school shooters. From Luke Woodham to Nikolas Cruz, male school shooters count being dumped as the last straw before enacting their plans to harm innocent students at their schools. Another school shooter that was rejected by a girl was Thomas Lane, from Chardon, Ohio.

Lane, 17, opened fire on his school in the Cleveland, Ohio area on February 27, 2012, during the first hour of school, which I call "the deadly hour." Lane pulled out a handgun in the cafeteria, shot five students, killing three and wounding two. The weapon used was a .22handgun, which the shooter obtained from his home, from possibly his uncle. He shot roughly ten rounds, beginning in the cafeteria. He stood up from a table and shot four male students, and as he ran from the school, shot a female student.

Lane had been posting threats on social media prior to the shooting, but those threats were not taken seriously. He targeted one student, and after the shooting was chased from the school by a teacher. Lane was arrested a short time later outside of the school and charged with numerous charges, including three counts of first degree murder. He was sentenced to three life sentences in the Ohio Department of Corrections, and his prison time has been very hard for him, including violent and sexual assaults. The time he was doing was so hard he actually escaped from prison with two other inmates but was apprehended the next day.

To answer the question of "why," one of the deceased victims had recently began dating the killer's former girlfriend and had threatened to beat up Lane. Fellow students stated that the killer targeted this male victim, as he was the first to be shot. The killer did not attend Chardon High School, but was attending an alternative school, and was waiting to be transported by bus to that school when the shooting occurred. Lane had made threats on social media, including Twitter and Facebook. One line read "Die all of you." Lane was obsessed with the show American Horror Story, which had a school shooting scene in an episode of its first season. Lane's causes include an unstable home life, no father, an obsession with violent entertainment, bullying, and possible mental illness. The warning signs were previous threats of violence, and the trigger seems to be a breakup with a girlfriend and reported bullying from one of the victims.

During his trial, he unbuttoned his dress shirt and removed it, unveiling a white t shirt with a handwritten message, "Killer." He also laughed and mocked the families of the victims during their victim impact statements, and when asked to speak, mumbled something like "the hand that pulled the trigger that killed your sons now masturbates to the memory...fuck all of you." He also flipped off the families and the courtroom.

2-PARENTS FORBIDDING A RELATIONSHIP WITH A GIRLFRIEND OR BOYFRIEND

When parents disapprove of their son or daughter's boyfriend or girlfriend, this can be a big let-down for teens and can spark anger and rage. Unfortunately, it can also act as a trigger for homicide or suicide. This is the number one trigger for female teen killers, pushing them to either kill on their own, or to team up with their lover and commit homicide. This was the trigger that caused Holly Harvey and Sandy Ketchum to murder Holly's grandparents in Georgia. It was also the trigger that caused Sarah Johnson to violently murder her own parents.

Diane and Scott Johnson, who lived in Bellevue, Idaho, disliked their daughter, Sarah's, 19-year-old boyfriend and advised her that she not only would end her dating relationship with him, but he would no longer be welcome at their home. In many instances, the daughter will team up with the boyfriend or girlfriend and murder her parents/ guardians or caregivers. But, in some cases, the daughter will kill her parents alone. That is exactly what happened in this violent double murder case. Sarah was not going to be told what to do, like many other members of her violent generation. And she chose murder as her solution.

On September 1, 2003, Sarah, 16, snuck into her parents' rental home and stole a loaded rifle from the renter. She snuck it back into her home and waited until the next morning to attack. On September 2, 2003, Sarah hatched her plan. She awoke at 6 am and marched into her parents' bedroom with her loaded rifle. Her mother was sound asleep, and her dad was already in the shower. She positioned the gun at her sleeping mother's head and pulled the trigger. A very loud explosion rocked the quiet home. When her father heard the loud noise, unsure what it was, he turned the shower off and opened the shower door, listening to the deafening silence.

Sarah then entered the bathroom and shot her father in the chest, dropped the weapon, and ran back into her bedroom, locking the door behind her. She then waited for her parents to die. Her mother was killed instantly, missing most of her head. Her father, with a large hole in his chest, stumbled to the phone in the bedroom but unfortunately succumbed to his injuries, falling and dying right next to the phone. Sarah then ran next door and told the neighbors to call the police, that someone had killed her parents while she was asleep.

Prior to running next door, Sarah cleaned up the crime scene, staged the scene as she imagined it should look and placed most of the evidence in a trash can. She discarded a robe she wore to keep the blood off her, rubber gloves full of her DNA, and other miscellaneous items. She flushed a shower cap down the toilet, which she wore during the bloody murders to keep the blood out of her hair. The police eventually located the evidence, connected her DNA to the crime scene evidence and charged her with two counts of first degree murder. Investigators didn't believe her story of an intruder killing her parents while she was asleep, and evidence proved she was not telling the truth. She was convicted and sentenced to life in prison, yet she continues to deny her guilt in the double murder.

Holly Harvey, 15, from Georgia, killed her grandparents when they told her she couldn't date her girlfriend, Sandy Ketchum. Harvey stabbed them to death in their home before fleeing to Tybee Island, Georgia.

3-SUSPENSION OR EXPULSION FROM SCHOOL

Many school shooters were expelled or suspended from school, which ended up being the trigger of their shootings. Kip Kinkel was expelled and arrested by police for having a gun in his locker, and he responded with a deadly school shooting. Parkland, Florida school killer Nikolas Cruz was expelled from school and he came back a year later to get his revenge, on February 14, 2018. This makes for a real quandary for schools, as they must act against students threatening other students, bullying other students, drawing violent pictures, or getting caught with drugs or even a hit list. They may or may not know that suspending or expelling students can be a trigger of homicide, but their hands are tied. They surely can't allow a violent student making threats to remain at the school.

For this reason, knowing this is a triggering event, I advise the school to contact law enforcement and the authorities before suspending or expelling a student, so everyone is on board, and proper precautions are taken. Some school shooters react within days of being suspended or expelled with violence, and few delay the attack, like Nikolas Cruz did. Schools will continue to do what they must do and should do to keep other students safe, and remove a threat, but I highly caution them to make sure parents, law enforcement, and counselors are also on board to do their part to prevent a possible tragedy.

4-BEING ARRESTED BY THE POLICE

Many teen killers and school shooters have no arrest record whatsoever, which shocks everyone including school administrators, friends and their own parents. But a history of being arrested can be a trigger for future homicide. Counselors, law enforcement and parents need to pay attention to smaller arrests for petty crimes, which can eventually escalate into homicide. Getting a juvenile who is going astray help, counseling, and to possible boot camps and schools where they can break their bad behaviors and learn to make better choices is a good idea. Sometimes being separated from bad influences and friends can help teens see their situation with better vision, helping them make better choices.

That is why I am proactive and supportive of rehabilitative schools and facilities where juveniles can be locked up for six to twelve months and receive intense counseling and therapy for a much longer term than being sent to a hospital for the weekend. The Columbine killers were arrested for petty theft and completed their probation shortly before the Columbine shooting.

5-DISPUTE WITH PARENTS

A dispute with parents over almost anything can be monumental to a teenager and could be a trigger. It could be a dispute or argument over curfew, use of a vehicle, rules in the home, video games, or the choice of a boyfriend or girlfriend. A major case that comes to mind when talking about this trigger is the case of Ohio gamer Danny Petric.

Daniel Petric, who went by Danny, was a normal teenager with a very stable family. His parents were youth workers at a local church, and he and his two sisters were loved by his parents and his grandparents, who lived next door. Along with playing sports and helping his father with yardwork, Danny had a penchant for violent video games. Being strict religious parents, the Petrics discouraged their son from playing violent video games that included the shooting and killing of human beings.

Danny's favorite game was Halo, and when the newest version of Halo came out, he had to have it. He snuck out one night, bought the game, and snuck it back into his home. Unfortunately for Danny, he was caught in the act and his parents took his Halo game from him. Locking it in his gun safe, Mark Petric advised his son that he would not be allowed to play that game in their home. One night, after locating the key to the gun safe, Danny opened the safe and removed his prized game, along with a .40 caliber handgun. He prepared to get even with his parents, using his newly acquired handgun as his weapon.

On October 20, 2007, a peaceful Sunday afternoon, when his parents were napping on the couch, Danny walked into the room, hiding the gun behind his back. He woke his parents from their naps, asking them to close their eyes and told them he had a surprise for them. Once they closed their eyes, he opened fire, first shooting his father in the back of the head and then shooting his mother multiple times, killing her. His father passed out from the shock and damage of the gunshot wound, but he woke up and survived the incident.

Danny fled in the family vehicle with his Halo game. He led police on a short chase and eventually surrendered. Instead of the arresting officers finding a weapon in the vehicle, they located a video game.

Danny made up a story that his father shot his mother and then himself, but the evidence said something different. Unfortunately for Danny, his father survived the shooting and would later tell police that his son shot him. Danny eventually confessed to the shooting and murder of his mother and was sentenced to 22 years in prison. Danny's father, Mark, made a full recovery and is supportive of his incarcerated son. Danny and his attorneys have claimed that violent video games played a key role and the World Health Organization has released a study to back up their claims.

6-MAJOR BULLYING INCIDENT AT SCHOOL

Bullying is not only a cause of teen murder and school shootings, but can act as a trigger as well. Barry Loukaitis and Dimitrios Pagoutzis both were triggered by a bullying incident. After being bullied for several months, Loukaitis was triggered to violence and opened fire at Frontier Middle School in Moses Lake, Washington. When a school bully called him a "faggot" in art class in front of the other students, he was pushed to violence. He told me, "After he said that, I decided at that very moment to kill him. And after ten days, I got him."

Pagoutzis opened fire at Santa Fe High School in Texas after being bullied for several months by students and teachers alike. When a female student embarrassed him in front of the entire class, telling him she would not date him, he decided to get even. He opened fire in an art class, killing ten people, including teachers and students. He also injured thirteen others before he was apprehended. A witness said he walked into art class holding a shotgun, wearing a trench coat, with a t-shirt with the words "Born to Kill." He pointed to one student and said "I'm going to kill you," and opened fire.

As a reminder, you usually need three to six of my causes of teen murder to be in the danger zone, which creates teen killers. Once in that zone, a violent teen who is planning on hurting someone will display some warning signs, at least one warning sign and as many as ten. But, even with the causes and warning signs, it takes a trigger to push a teenager to become a killer. Usually, those triggers are the ones I listed in this chapter. Remember, most teen killers and school shooters plan for six, twelve, and even up to eighteen months, so you will have a chance to see the warning signs, causes, and triggers, and hopefully get them help before it's too late.

CHAPTER FIVE
VIOLENT AND OBSCENE TEEN ENTERTAINMENT

"The media is the catalyst that pushes them over the edge"
-Greg McCrary, FBI Criminal Profiler

"You can't have the kind of saturation of violence that we have today
without it manifesting itself somewhere. It's like a virus spreading
through a large population of people. Not everyone gets sick. Just
the most vulnerable, and then with varying degrees of illness."
-Dewey Cornell, Director, University of
Virginia Youth Violence Project

At a bipartisan congressional conference in 2000, the medical
community, which included the American Medical Association and
the American Academy of Pediatrics, submitted a joint statement
that read:

"At this time, well over one thousand studies...point overwhelmingly
to a causal connection between media violence and the aggressive behavior
in some children. The conclusion of the public health community,
based on over thirty years of research, is that viewing entertainment
violence can lead to increases in aggressive attitudes, values and behavior,
particularly in children." And pertaining to video games, "Preliminary
studies indicate that the negative impact may be significantly more severe
than that wrought by television, movies and music."

-American Academy of Pediatrics "Joint Statement on the Impact of Entertainment Violence on Children Congressional Public Health Summit, July 26, 2000

MUSIC

The music of today is about as raw and violent as we have ever witnessed, with some of the biggest artists rapping and singing about rape, torture and murder. What is even worse are the videos the artists create to promote their music. When rapper 21 Savage raps in his song "All The Smoke," he boasts, "Gotta keep that pistol on me...shoot em in the face, shoot em in the nose...AR with the scope, nigga don't get close...I'm cutthroat nigga, swiss blade...closed casket nigga, I'm a bastard." In this video, he killed two women, beheaded one, threw her head in the woods, and smashed the other's head in with a hammer in an extremely violent fashion.

Rapper David Banner rails against the police and racism in his song "Black Fist," and in his music video, he hangs a police officer, stabs him and drowns him, basically comparing the police to the KKK. Two Chains also bashes the police in his song "I'm Different," and the video has civilians pulling over a police officer, planting drugs on him, arresting him at gunpoint, insinuating that the police plant drugs on civilians.

Pop sensation Rhianna, today's version of Madonna, performs a song titled "Bitch Better Have My Money," and the video is downright shocking. She kidnaps a white female and hangs her by her feet in a warehouse, in just her underwear, with no bra. Viewers assume she murders her because Rhianna shows several weapons of murder, including a chainsaw and knives. The video ends with Rhianna laying naked in a trunk, covered in blood, and covered in her money. In my opinion, I am stunned that women's groups aren't calling for a boycott of Rhianna's video and demanding a public apology, as it glorifies the abuse and murder of women.

Cardi B, one of the hottest pop musicians of her day, rapped on a song "Press" about killing rivals, displayed in full horror in her music video. She boasts in the song "Cardi don't need more press, Kill em' all, put them hoes to rest...murder scene, Cardi made a mess...guess who, bitch?"

Two of the more violent musicians with a large following are Eminem and Insane Clown Posse, whose music lyrics are among the most violent in the industry. Eminem has multiple violent songs dating back several years, including "Kim," "Bonnie and Clyde," and "Criminal." On the song "3AM," he raps "It's 3AM in the morning, put my key in the door and bodies layin' all over the floor...I don't remember how they got there, but I guess I must've killed them." The video for this song is also very violent, in which he stabs a nurse to death in a hospital. In the song "Kill You," Eminem boasts "Slut, you won't think I won't choke no whore, til the vocal cords don't work in her throat no more...Texas Chainsaw, left his brains all dangling from his neck, while his head barely hangs on...Bitch, I'ma kill you...conceal you in a closet...and film you...just like criminal intent to sodomize women again...Shady will fucking kill you."

The violent horrorcore group Insane Clown Posse, who although are not mainstream, have a very large underground following. Their fans, the Juggalos, have committed so many crimes including murder, rape and various violent crimes that the FBI labeled their fans as a hybrid gang. Their lyrics contain a slew of graphic and violent content, including murder, suicide, and assault. In the song "Chicken Huntin," they rap "I'ma cut his neck up...cut his fucking eyes out and feed em to his Aunt Millie...hit him with the twelve gauge...laid all over the grass...barrels in your mouth, bullets to your head, the back of your neck is all over the shed."

MOVIES

There are and have been many horror movies about murder and bloodshed over the last few decades, but today's movies seem to up the ante when it comes to realistic violence. Of the worst released in the last decade, torture films seem to offer the most torture, graphic violence and death. The Saw movie series is one of the most popular torture film series. In what some call "torture porn," this film has six installments to date and was released annually around Halloween. The film basically consists of creative ways to torture and kill people, and most of the films run for two hours. One reviewer, Steven Isaac from Plugged In Magazine, described Saw III as "There is no end to the ways in which these movies can show people being mangled, lacerated, dissected, brutalized...and murdered." The last film was released in 2009, but they remain a pinnacle and set the bar for torture films, which are rated R, meaning older teens can attend these bloodfests legally.

Another torture film series is the Hostel series, which had three installments. This movie series is about two college students traveling across Europe who are preyed upon by a group of killers who kidnap, torture and kill backpackers. The murders and dismemberment are extremely graphic and the tools of torture include knives, chainsaws, and other various deadly weapons. The victims' bodies are skinned, hanged, butchered, burned and mutilated. This is the ultimate example of gore porn, including a clip I show in my live training, taken from Hostel 2. In this clip, a naked female is hanged, and a naked woman lies below her in an empty bathtub so when she cuts and slices into her flesh, the blood drips onto her body, sending her into a sexual frenzy, as she smear the fresh blood all over her body.

This scene continues on for a few minutes, and it ends when the woman below grabs a sickle and slices her victim's throat, killing her as she bleeds out all over her killer, sending the female killer into an orgasm. Other violent torture films include Final Destination, The Texas Chainsaw Massacre, The Purge, The Last House on the Left, Wrong Turn 2, and The Poughkeepsie Tapes.

A film that has been mentioned by school shooters is Oliver Stone's Natural Born Killers, which was a big inspiration to the Columbine Killers. They actually named their shooting "NBK," an abbreviation of this movie's name. Two movies have been made about Columbine, and teens who had planned school violence have mentioned these two movies. The 2003 movie Elephant, which is said to have inspired the Red lake school shooting, and the 2004 movie Zero Day.

As you may or may not know, these types of movies are extremely accessible to today's teens. Not only can they purchase a PG ticket and walk into an R rated movie, but they can rent and purchase these movies online and in the movie vending machine Redbox.

VIDEO GAMES

As I begin this discussion about video games, remember there are no laws in place to protect children from the violent and sexual content in video games like there is in place for the movie industry and pornography. There are suggested ratings, but they are not enforced by the government or law enforcement. The ratings that video game manufacturers add to the cover of the game are as follows: E means everyone, and these games are safe for kids, which includes games like Mario Cart and Donkey Kong. Rated T for teens can be safe, but can also have some violent content. Rated M means Mature 17+ and these games are not safe or recommended for younger children or teens. Manhunt, Saints Row and Grand Theft Auto are all rated M and have extremely violent content. The AO rating means Adults Only 18+, and these games are usually filled with extreme violence and/or realistic pornography. An example of an AO game would be the killing game Hatred.

Let's review some of the violent video games that have influenced children for the last twenty-five years, and how it has impacted our society. If you remember, video games began to emerge in the 1970's and 1980's with games like Pong, PacMan, Donkey Kong and Asteroids. Some of the first hints of violence began in 1987 with Street Fighter, which allowed you to fight against opponents. In the 1970's and 1980's, we had teen violence and teen murder, but we were not yet experiencing juvenile mass murder or school massacres, as we call them today. During these decades, teens would walk into a school and shoot their bully or shoot their girlfriend who just broke up with them. At the most, a school shooting up until 1993 consisted of one or two victims.

In 1992 things changed in the United States, as the video game industry felt it was a good idea to begin teaching children to kill. Beginning in 1992 and 1993, game manufacturers began releasing first person shooter video games, where the goal is killing, and you get rewarded points for doing so. In 1992, we saw the release of Duke Nukem, Night Trap, Lethal Enforcers and Mortal Combat. In 1993, the release of the first-person shooter game Doom set the stage for many shooting games to follow, including Grand Theft Auto.

In Duke Nukem and Doom, both first person shooting games, you get rewarded for killing people with points. The Columbine killers loved these two games and mentioned them in their journals and manifestos. In the game Night Trap, a game that features violence and sexual aggression against women, you can watch simulated video of women at a sleepover, where they are violently attacked. It is very similar to watching a real live video. The "nightgown scene" from Night Trap was raised by Congress as an example of video game violence, in which a woman has her blood drained. Lethal Enforcers is a shooting game that allows you to kill enemies and is one of the first games rated M. Mortal Kombat was an early violent video game that featured blood spray and graphic violence, with fatality finishes. Remember the words "Finish Him?" Gamers could kill their enemies in very violent ways including pulling someone's spine out of their body or removing their head, which was not common at that point in video game development.

The next wave of games in the 1990's brought us a plethora of increasingly violent titles, more than their predecessors, including Grand Theft Auto, Carmegeddon and Thrill Kill. In Carmageddon, released in 1997, which is known as "the racing game for the chemically imbalanced," this game allows you to run people over, killing them in an ultra-bloody fashion. In Thrill Kill, released in 1998, the content is sexually charged and violent, including sadomasochistic content and the removal of your enemies' limbs. But the granddaddy of violent video games, which has probably spawned the most amount of real-life violence, is the Grand Theft Auto series, which was first released in 1997. Grand Theft Auto gameplay includes picking up and having graphic sex with prostitutes and killing them when you are done to get your money back. You can even take pictures of their dead bodies and set them on fire. The game glorifies torture, murder, gun violence, drug dealing, contract killing, the murder of police officers, drunk driving, strip clubs, pornographic sex scenes, and street crime.

In the early 2000's, we saw the release of several more violent, first person shooter games, or killing simulators, which gave the player points for killing human beings. In the 2000 game Soldier of Fortune, the technology allows you to torture your victims in a realistic fashion, blowing their limbs off with a shotgun, and blowing someone's guts out. In the Halo series, launched in 2001, you are killing alien type beings in a military science fiction setting. There are segments where you can kill other humans, and this game was involved in an Ohio teen murder case, the case of family killer Daniel Petric.

In 2003, Manhunt was released, and Manhunt 2 was released in 2007. This game has been banned in several countries and for good reason. You can kill your victims in horrific fashion, with about any weapon you can think of, from the typical gun, knife and axe, to the plastic bag and electric saw. Even the staff at Rockstar Games were uncomfortable with the level of violence in this game, as former employee Jeff Williams stated that it was so violent that it made the staff uncomfortable and "made us all feel icky...We all knew there was no way we could explain away that game. There was no way to rationalize it. We were crossing a line." (7/26/07, GamesRadar).

In 2003, Postal 2 was released, and this game has some depraved acts of violence that few games have, like using a cat's corpse as a silencer, as you stick your gun up its anus. You can also hit people with decapitated cow heads, and you can use severed human heads to play fetch with dogs. Also, in one of the sickest acts in a video game, you can urinate on the corpse of your dead victim. Other violent games to follow were Call of Duty in 2003, Saints Row in 2006, and God of War 2 in 2007. In God of War 2, the violence and gore are realistic, including slamming a door on another God's head, complete with a tremendous amount of blood, gore and finishing kills. In 2008, Gears of War 2 came out, and this blood-soaked game allows you to slice people with a chainsaw and use a corpse as a human shield. In 2009, Madworld was released, which is a slasher game with numerous acts of realistic and graphic violence, gore, and blood.

Some of the newer, lesser known video games include: Bulletstorm: Full Clip Edition, which contains blood, gore, and dismemberment. Conan Exiles, which contains blood, gore, dismemberment, and decapitation. Dark Souls 3: The Ringed City, allows you to slash and impale with plenty of blood and gore. Dead by Daylight is a slasher game that allows the player to hack, stab, impale and hang victims on meat hooks. For Honor includes blood and placing severed heads on spikes. Friday the 13th: The Game, contains blood, gore and sexualized violence. Outlast 2 includes blood, gore, torture and stabbing. Player Unknown's Battleground allows the player to kill with cars, melee weapons or bare hands.

Other games parents should be aware of, which contain graphic acts of sex and violence include: Scarface, The World Is Yours, True Crime: Streets Of LA, Watch Dogs, Sleeping Dogs, Just Cause, Mafia, and The Godfather. In 2015, an Adults Only game was released called Hatred, and in my opinion, is a sign of things to come. The game features a ruthless mass murderer of innocent people, mostly police officers and members of the military, in the most brutal fashion. You can shoot multiple victims to death with a rifle, set people on fire, curb stomp your victims, and stab random victims in the throat, eye and temple. One of the most shocking ways to kill people is when you grab them by the hair, stick a handgun in their mouth and blow their brains out. When you use the shotgun, it blows their head off completely. This game is rated AO for adults only, but teens will be able to get their hands on it, because it is an internet platform video game.

One last thing I need to address is the popular 2017 game Fortnite, which is a survival action game where you battle others and fight to the death. You use melee weapons and kill others, but the violence is more "cartoonish." It would be like combining Minecraft with Call of Duty and although cartoonish, there are a lot of guns and violence. My take on this game is this: I'd rather have your child playing Fortnite over Grand Theft Auto. But I'd also rather have your child playing Madden Football over Fortnite.

HELPFUL RESOURCES

To keep up with teen entertainment and youth culture, I recommend the following websites:

1. Azlyrics.com: A great lyric search engine.
2. Covenanteyes.com: A porn accountability service for those young people struggling with a porn addiction.
3. XXXChurch.com: A pornography accountability website for those struggling with a porn addiction.
4. Ohhla.com: The Original Hip-Hop Lyric Archive, featuring rap lyrics of almost every rapper in history
5. Pluggedin.com: This faith-based website features reviews of movies, music, television shows, video games and books.
6. Protectyoungeyes.com: Help your children navigate social media and phone apps.
7. Screenit.com: Movie reviews (possibly subscription based).
8. Urbandictionary.com: A great site to look up the latest sayings of teens, like Thot, Ratchet and Getting Neck.
9. Worldstarhiphop.com: An urban website that I use to keep up with current events and youth culture. The site is very biased and one-sided, and anti-police, but I check in daily to keep up with current events, the rap scene, and teen trends. Warning, there is nudity, sex, violence, fights, and plenty of obscenity.

CHAPTER SIX
DANGEROUS SOCIAL MEDIA, PHONE APPS AND PORNOGRAPHY

SOCIAL MEDIA AND PHONE APPS

1. 4Chan.com: This website can be a dangerous place for teens, with its sexual images, disturbing material, and depraved information. You can remain anonymous, and you don't have to create an account, which allows users to say and post whatever content they want, and nobody knows who you really are.

2. After School: This app allows your teens to post anonymously and see things that other teens post. Like many apps, you can expect bullying, gossiping, sexting, and making fun of teachers, police officers, principals and fellow students.

3. Ask.fm: This app allows teens to create an account, connect with friends, and meet new people by asking and answering questions. This can connect your child with strangers, and some may have bad intentions. Although this app doesn't include pornography, there are links that can take the user to pornography. There has been a lot of cyber bullying reported from users of this app.

4. Badoo.com: This website and social media platform is a dating service used by 180 million people. Your children can be exposed to adult content, bullying, nudity and sexual content.

5. Blendr: A hook-up sex app that allows you to connect with locals, and marketers use the words "chat, flirt and meet" to describe this app. It is also described as "free, socially flirtatious chat to meet app. The app will let you know when you're near another user, and displays their face, which can be troubling and dangerous. You can also enter a "singles chat room," where the risk of obscene and sexually charged conversations are not only possible, but probable. Lastly, there is no information verification, so there is no way to know if a person is who they say they are in the app.

6. Bumble: This is a location-based dating platform (similar to Tinder) that allows women to make the first move and encourages them to make the first contact. In same sex connections, either can make the first move. When a match is made between strangers, you have twenty-four hours to begin the conversation, or the match expires. As an app that encourages strangers to make a love connection, it is potentially dangerous and life-threatening for teens and children.

7. Chat Roulette: This is a website that accesses your webcam and microphone, and pairs you up with a random person to have a video chat with. Knowing the type of people that might utilize these social media platforms, this is a big problem for your children. Chat Roulette is known for nudity, like grown men masturbating live, exposing themselves, and adults who want to have sex chats.

8. Digital Scale Pro: This app turns your mobile phone into a scale, weighing items in grams or ounces. This would allow your child to weigh drugs right on his or her phone. If your teen has a digital scale on their phone, you might want to start asking questions.

9. Down: A dating app that is really designed for people to meet and have casual sex. This is a sex hook-up app.

10. Dubsmash: This is an app used to create videos in which you can dub audio over top of the video from other sources, like movies or songs. Some of the movie or song content might be

sexual or violent in nature. This app can be fun for children, if the content is monitored.

11. Find My Friends: This app allows users to track each other's locations using the GPS on their phones. Once again, danger presents itself when your child shares this app with others, allowing others, some with fake accounts, to track their location at all times. Once located on a map, simply click on "more" and get the exact address of their location.

12. Foursquare: This app allows users to "check in" at various locations and receive rewards for doing so. Since this app locates you, your child can be in danger if they continue to check in at various locations, allowing strangers to stalk them and possibly harm them.

13. Hide It Pro: This app allows your children to hide their apps from you, so you have no idea what apps they are using, and what kind of danger they might be in.

14. Holla: An app that matches users with complete strangers, and the content includes plenty of nudity and pornography.

15. Hot or Not: An app for dating and meeting new people, with many using fake accounts to trick users. This app can connect your child to a dangerous adult with a fake profile, and meeting a stranger on this platform could be very dangerous and possibly fatal.

16. Kik or Kik Messenger: An app that provides a messaging service over a cellular data network or with an internet connection. There have been cases of teens talking to strangers thinking they were talking to young people, and some teens have been kidnapped and murdered. This app is like texting on a cell phone, and you don't need cell service or a phone number. This allows your child to text strangers without you knowing it. Your teens can be messaging people who are not who they say they are, and if they decide to meet in real life, it can lead to fatal consequences.

17. Ky-Calc Calculator: This app hides photos and videos on mobile phones and other mobile devices in the guise of a regular

calculator, so parents can't see them. Think porn, hit lists, and school shooting plans.

18. Lipsi: A feedback app that breeds bullying and harassment.

19. Live.Me: This is a social media platform that allows teens to live stream videos from the comfort of their bedrooms. It was reported that girls as young as ten years old are using this app to promote sexual behaviors. They dance, strip, and ask their viewers what they want to see next. They get rewarded with virtual currency and other perks in what some are calling a "pedophile's paradise." It has also been reported that some viewers film this content and sell it to child pornography websites.

20. Muimeet: An GPS location-based match dating app. It advertises as having the ability for live flirting. Once again, many use fake accounts to trick other users. This app can connect your child to a dangerous adult with a fake profile and meeting a stranger on this platform could be fatal, or very dangerous at the least.

21. Omegle: With a tagline and marketing campaign that states "talk to strangers," this app pairs you with complete strangers, some obviously with bad intentions. Depending on the stranger, your children could experience naked men and/or women, bullying and aggressive behavior

22. Periscope: This is a live streaming app that allows teens to broadcast live video from their bedrooms, and in turn, allows complete strangers to chat with them. Subscribers of Periscope can "look in" on anyone streaming a video, and the teen who is making the live video has no idea who is watching behind their profile and screen. Users have experienced a lot of negatives from chatting with strangers, which includes bullying, peer pressure, and sexual banter. The worst feature about the app is that the user who is streaming a live video can be located on an interactive and detailed map. This puts not only the teen in danger, but also his or her family, should a psychopath want to cause harm.

23. Phhhoto: An image app that allows the user to connect multiple images together to create something that resembles a gif or video. Your teens can connect with other users, and the content and photos they might observe are out of your control and can be sexual or obscene in nature. Dangers include chatting with adult users unsupervised, the viewing of inappropriate images, and possibly meeting up with strangers, which can possibly lead to fatal consequences.

24. Photo Vault: This app hides photos and videos on mobile phones and other mobile devices so others and guardians/parents can't see them. Think porn, hit lists, and school shooting plans.

25. Poof: This app operates under the same premise as "Hide It Pro". It allows your children to hide their apps from you, so you have no idea what apps they are using, and what kind of danger they might be in.

26. Secret: An anonymous messaging board that allows users to post things without regret or consequences. It is banned in some countries, and it has five million users. Expect bullying, hate speech, sexual content, obscenity, sexting, nudity, and more.

27. Snapchat: Formerly a sexting app that allowed sexually explicit photos to disappear, has become mainstream, and most teens are now loyal users. The main danger of this platform is you can be located while using the app. Along with Instagram, it's one of the two more popular social media platforms used by teens.

28. Snapsave and Casper: Allows you to save images from other users without them knowing. This is not only dangerous, but also illegal if the images are pornographic in nature.

29. Tagged.com: An app for dating and meeting new people. It also touts itself as an app to play games with over 300 million users. This app can connect your child to a dangerous adult with a fake profile and meeting a stranger on this platform could be very dangerous.

30. Tinder: This is an app for dating and meeting new people, and many use fake accounts to trick users. This app can connect your child to a dangerous adult with a fake profile and meeting

a stranger on this platform could be fatal, or very dangerous at the least.

31. Whisper: This app is basically an online message board where users can upload messages anonymously. And only people that live relatively close to you can see these messages, so you are interacting with local people. The app allows you to post your deepest and darkest secrets, and users can send direct messages to the person posting, which can lead to bullying and an unwanted message from a predator. This app allows cyber bullying to take place, and several schools have mentioned this app as a problem.

32. Wishbone: An app that was launched in 2015 and describes itself as "the go-to for comparing anything your heart desires." Because it is a survey-based app, children can use it to compare each other, which can result in cyber-bullying. If connected to other platforms like Facebook, too much information can be gathered about its users, which can lead to dangerous situations. Predators can groom young people and gain their trust using this app, which could have fatal consequences. Users can private message each other in this app, which can be hidden from parents' view.

33. Yellow: This app allows users to see pictures and profile information of other users who live near them, and like Tinder, if a user likes your profile and swipes right, the two can connect. If they both swipe right, their snapchats are connected and they can exchange pictures. This has been called "Tinder for Teens," and obviously can be dangerous when teens are connecting and meeting local strangers.

34. Younow: This app allows users to stream live video, which obviously can pose a problem for both users and viewers. Sexual content, nudity, and bullying are all possible here.

35. Zepeto: This app allows users to interact with strangers, with no privacy

There are several anonymous messaging apps out there, and new ones are created every single day. Other notable dangerous messaging apps include Chatible, Tick Chat, Turtle, and Secret So Far.

Other apps parents should be concerned about or aware of: Bigo Live, Blendr, Burn Book, Discord, Slingshot, Tellonym, Tik Tok, Yeti and Yik Yak.

Another concern for parents are devices like ROKU, Infinity, or Fire stick, which allows children and teens to stream live movies, television shows and more in the comfort of their homes, on their devices, computers and personal TVs. If parents don't set up a pin number for parental controls, it would be easy to download and watch inappropriate content and/or porn videos all day and night.

PORNOGRAPHY

Another concern for parents is the kind of content that is available to children and teens today via the Internet. One of my biggest concerns is internet pornography. Some of the latest stats and studies claim 10% of today's porn users are under the age of ten years old. Imagine a five-year-old looking at a man having anal sex with a woman? Imagine what that would do to his or her social/emotional development. I find that young children who are exposed to internet porn at an early age display signs like children being molested, as they are actually being visually sexually assaulted by internet porn. So, when I say the word "pornography," what comes to mind for you? Maybe you imagine naked men and women, or a couple having traditional sex. But today's porn is nothing like that. Instead, it is orgies, anal sex, physical violence, masturbating into a woman's face, torture, and more.

I was getting my wife ready to teach in Florida schools, and basically training her on warning signs of violence, and today's youth culture. She had never seen porn before, so I told her I wanted her to experience what her students would be seeing for hundreds of hours per year. I started out with a mainstream porn website, which I will not mention, but everyone knows it, as it is featured on Instagram, Facebook and Internet memes.

Once on that site, I showed her that you can choose whatever kind of sex you like, be it anal, blondes, ebony or black females, bukkake, or climaxing into a woman's face, and more. When you click "teens", you get introduced to kiddie porn, and when you choose hardcore, you venture into more of the torture porn. We chose hardcore, and with one click, we dropped into a torture porn site, with a similar name to "torture teens." I won't reveal the exact website address, but it was a very sick and disturbing website. We watched a stepfather anally rape his stepdaughter on the back of a pickup truck and were shocked as it was one click from a mainstream porn website. Very troubling indeed.

Because of this, I would sternly warn parents to begin a new rule-to make a norm in their homes- No devices in their teen's bedrooms at night. Make your child's bedroom a device-free zone at night, allowing them to study and sleep in peace and quiet. This helps to eliminate the risk of talking to strange people, broadcasting live video from your home, and looking at sick and violent pornography. If your teens are angry, blame me and explain that a study has been released about teens and sleep patterns, and eliminating these devices will help them sleep better. Allow them to play their video games and listen to music and watch television until their bedtime, but eliminate their connected devices throughout the night. Charge their device in your master bedroom, and the best news of all, your kids might sleep better, be more alert at school, and raise their grades and test scores.

HELPFUL RESOURCES

Here are a few of my personal recommended resources for helping your teens navigate through dangerous social media and pornographic websites:

1. iparent.tv: This is a very cool website that allows you to learn about dangerous phone apps, social media platforms, and more. This is how I keep up with dangerous teen social media apps

and programs, and it is brought to us by Craig Gross, founder of XXXChurch, described below.

2. CovenantEyes.com: This a great tool for those addicted to violent pornography and allows the user to obtain accountability, which is the key to conquering an internet porn addition. The addiction to pornography is like a crack cocaine addiction and is very hard to kick. This tool will assist your child to take control and beat this addiction. If the porn addiction continues, possible consequences are guilt, depression, suicide, and even the need for Viagra. Viagra has become a prescription for younger and younger men, as seeing pornography repeatedly can make it tough to have sex with a real person. We also know that a lifetime addiction to porn can cost you a marriage, relationships with children and loved ones and can affect your career as well.

3. XXXChurch.com: This is another great tool for those addicted to pornography and allows the user to obtain accountability. As I said before, accountability is the key to conquering a pornography addiction.

4. Mymobilewatchdog.com: Like teensafe.com, this platform is geared more for younger people, like your twelve-year-old when they get their first phone. They know this app is on their phone, but if they are younger, they won't mind. It allows you to control their phone, inspecting their photo texts, blocking dangerous apps from working on their phone, and allowing you to shut their phone down at your discretion. You also are always able to track their GPS location. Great tool for younger teens, but older teens will not like this and probably obtain another cell phone if this software is on their device.

5. MSPY.com: mSpy is a leading parental control app for smartphones that allows parents to monitor text messages, calls, current GPS location, Snapchat, WhatsApp and much more.

CHAPTER SEVEN
SCHOOL SAFETY

When it comes to keeping our students, teachers and staff safe at school, everyone has an opinion on the best method. Every single time there is a school shooting or mass murder, people from all walks of life come out of the woodwork, become experts and proclaim to know the answer to stopping mass tragedies. Politicians use these tragedies to further their policies and agendas, and the mainstream media use these events to attract viewers resulting in profit, as well as using these incidents to further push their biased agendas and opinions. Meanwhile, the conservatives, liberals, Democrats and Republicans attack each other, claiming THEY have the right answer. Sadly, this political posturing begins shortly after the taking of innocent lives, and before the crime scene clean-up has begun.

So, what is the correct response? Are there real, common sense answers and solutions? Should we ban guns? Should we ban the AR-15 rifle? Is it about assault rifles and multiple round magazines? Should we be doing a better job at treating the mentally ill? Is it the President's fault? Is the National Rifle Association to blame? How about the spread of violent video games and youth entertainment? Maybe it's the breakdown of family? Others would say it all began when God was kicked out of school, and prayer was eliminated. So, what is the answer? Can we sift through all these responses and come up with a real solution? I will do my best to do just that.

I would bet that of all the solutions, one of them must be something you believe in. I will say that I hate politics, despise biased news media, and rail against hate and division. So, I will do my best to drop politics and remain neutral, and honestly stick to the facts and the truth about school safety and the welfare of our children, our most precious assets. As I do this, please keep in mind that I am not a politician, nor am I am member of the media. I also am not an active police officer, so I have an unbiased agenda. What I do is interview real-life killers and report the findings. After over 200 interviews, a pattern does emerge. I also get a behind-the-scenes look at school shootings and mass murders being a law enforcement and homicide trainer. With that in mind, let me give you my educated opinion on how we, as a society, can stop these mass tragedies.

After doing this work for 35 years, studying all the FBI and Secret Service reports, and working closely with police, detectives and the homicide teams who have worked these incidents, I have a few thoughts on how we can keep our schools safe. Newsweek Magazine called me "The Teen Killer Whisperer" for a reason, and that reason is I can get inside the mind of a teen killer and school shooter, and interpret why they did that they did, and how they accomplished it. This kind of information helps us prevent future tragedies and stop many teen killers and school shooters before they shoot or stab innocent people. I would ask that you keep an open mind, in the spirit of helping children, and listen to what I have to say. Let's steer clear of biases and agendas and simply look at the facts. Thank you for caring about today's children!

If I were to ask you what you think we should do to stop school shootings and mass murders, what would you say? Another question I would ask you is, "Why are some school shootings and mass murderers deadlier than others?" Here is what we know: Most school shooters and mass murderers have a plan to commit suicide, so consequences of incarceration don't prevent these incidents. Most school shooters and mass murderers attack soft targets, or gun free zones, because they don't want resistance, especially trained law enforcement shooting back at them.

The main goal of a mass killer today is a high body count, or a high score. When the police are not present, and guns are not allowed, the killer knows they have between five and fifteen minutes before the police arrive to snuff out as many lives as possible. They know that more dead victims equal more fame, thanks to our mainstream media. They will bring a deadly weapon, either a gun or a knife. Or they might use bombs, explosives or fire. And they need a lot of targets. The best places to attack are locations where numerous people are gathered and there are no guns present. This would be what we call a "gun-free zone." Think schools, movie theaters, churches, malls, sporting events, or any place a good size crowd of people assemble.

As far as acquiring weapons, most teen killers, school shooters and mass murderers can acquire their weapons with little problem. Adult killers usually purchase their weapons legally, as it is extremely difficult in our society to brand someone "mentally ill," making it illegal for them to purchase weapons. Regarding teen killers and school shooters-juveniles who are too young to legally purchase weapons, they usually acquire them in one of three ways: They steal them, they purchase stolen weapons, or they get them from home. My point is current gun laws and more gun laws don't stop school shootings and mass murders, as killers don't follow gun laws. If a person wants to kill someone, they will obtain the weapon they need. Some teens resort to baseball bats, crow bars, kitchen knives, and axes. I believe in and support our current gun laws, but I don't think they will stop school shootings.

Banning weapons will never happen in America, as it would have the same effect as prohibition. Gang violence currently accounts for 70% of gun murders in America today, and we all know gang members do not follow the established laws of our nation. Should we attempt to ban weapons, gang members would shift from selling street drugs to selling guns. The profit they would see from this underground criminal enterprise would be unprecedented. So, since we can't stop the killers from obtaining weapons, we must harden our targets, like other countries do. Very few school shootings or mass murders have taken place where there were police officers or armed security.

The biggest solution we hear from students, politicians and the mainstream media is gun control, and specifically banning AR-15 rifles, or "assault rifles" as some call them. They also tone it down by asking for "common sense gun laws" and "tougher gun laws." The gun laws we have in place are already tough, and background checks are required on purchases. There are also requirements that need to be followed, such as you must be a certain age to purchase a gun, and you can't be diagnosed mentally ill. For a gun purchase, there is a waiting period and if you purchase a gun at a gun show, you also must pass the background check. You can ban the AR-15, but less than 10% of mass murderers prefer that gun, most using handguns. As a gun owner, I support gun laws. But I realize that guns can be purchased illegally on the street, and online, and nobody would know. The same could be said for rifles, high capacity magazines, bump stocks and silencers.

I personally own guns for protection, and I am not the stereotypical gun owner. I don't own 50 guns, I don't shoot every weekend, and I am not a member of the NRA. I joke that I would always much rather carry a cop, but they are heavy and not always available when I need them. So instead, I carry a firearm. If I could afford armed security every time I went out, like politicians and celebrities do, I would not need guns. But I cannot afford that luxury, so I arm myself. This is called being proactive and prepared.

Also, if we were able to rid America of all guns, which would probably take 50 to 100 years, killers would just move to other weapons, like knives, cars or explosives. London, which is about the size of New York City, does not allow guns, but had more murders this year than New York City. Many countries that outlaw guns have plenty of murders, either by knives or illegal guns. Remember, 9/11 was done by airplanes, and Oklahoma City was done by a bomb made from fertilizer. Guns need to be regulated, which the government is doing, but getting them out of the hands of would-be killers is a tall task. Maybe if we stopped glamorizing guns in entertainment, from video games to movies, television shows to rap videos, young people might possibly be less fascinated with them. And maybe if we would stop making these killers famous and making them as big a household name as the President, entertainers or movie stars, maybe they would not be so motivated to kill others when they want to kill themselves.

Another solution many are offering is treating the mentally ill, which

I feel is a very needed solution. But how do we identify the mentally ill? And who is going to diagnose a mentally ill person and confine them to a lockdown facility? And where are these facilities located, since many have been closed over the last 40 years? Most mentally ill people don't request help, so they will not seek treatment on their own. And with our politically correct society, hurting someone's feelings will always trump getting someone the help they need. Treating mental illness as a solution is a noble one. Yet, treating the mentally ill today before they kill is extremely difficult. As you all know, most of our mentally ill citizens are either homeless or in prison, which is very sad. Forty years ago, the mentally ill were locked up in facilities which kept them in a safe place for treatment, and kept the public protected as well.

Others, who are more politically biased in nature, want to blame politicians and political parties, as well as political organizations. From President Trump to President Obama, Hillary Clinton to Bernie Sanders, Republicans to Democrats, and the NRA and the group, Everytown For Gun Safety. For starters, there is no proof that a President or politician is responsible for a mass murder. School shootings, mass murders and terrorist attacks have happened under republican and democrat presidents, and have happened under the watch of Presidents Trump, Obama, Bush and Clinton.

Others point to the increase of media violence, especially the entertainment aimed at today's teens. While I agree that this could help, this in and of itself is not the answer. But with profit as king in America, and greedy companies defending their actions with the second amendment, I don't see much changing with this influence. When a game manufacturer like Rock Star Games can make $800 million in the first day from a violent video game like Grand Theft Auto 5 and has made $6 billion in revenue since its initial release, stopping these negative influences would have to take a major decision from Congress and the upper echelons of our government. Violent media manufacturers have the best attorneys, lobby the most influential politicians, and pay the best doctors and psychologists to conduct studies that prove their product doesn't negatively affect children.

Last, there are people that say the only solution is to allow God and prayer back into school. Although I don't think this would hurt anyone, I don't ever see this happening again. With the multitude of negative influences surrounding our children, this would likely be shadowed by the other influences. Case in point, teen murder and school shootings have happened at private and religious schools, where prayer is a daily part of the students' curriculum.

So, what is my professional opinion on how to stop school shootings and mass murders, and keep our children safe? There are two things a school shooter and mass murderer need: Time to kill people, and easy access to victims. Most of this chapter will be about school safety, but concerning mass murder in places like malls, churches and movie theaters, you need armed law enforcement present, and you need to do your best to lock doors and make victims as hard to get to as possible. But we are more focused on school safety in this chapter, so here is the quick answer to school massacres.

You must have an armed police officer present in every school, with a marked police car out in front of the building, announcing to all who might do harm to your students that they will receive return gunfire from a police officer. Potential killers don't like the threat of an armed law enforcement officer and would rather attack a building with no law enforcement. Second, the school shooter needs easy access to victims, be it at an assembly, in a lunchroom, or inside classrooms. Lockdown drills help with a plan in the event of a shooting but locking your classroom doors all day long prevents a gunman from entering a classroom, trapping innocent students, and murdering them with ease. So, until the government takes real action toward keeping our children safe, which we will discuss next, you must have armed law enforcement in your buildings, lock your exterior doors, and always lock all your interior classroom doors. Locking doors is an easy first line of defense and doesn't stretch school budgets or require extra personnel.

A lot of people are screaming at the President, politicians, and the government to do something about school shootings. And rightly so. But I always ask those people when given the chance, what they think the President should do? Or better yet, why they are blaming the President? Usually, exasperated, they just want these shootings to stop, and they want the government and politicians to do something. So, let's walk through it. Murder is illegal, so that is in place. It is illegal to bring a gun to school, so that law is in place. Schools are doing their best, with their limited budgets, to keep their students safe. And on average, we still have between five and ten school shootings per year. Now, that is not a lot, considering how many schools there are in America, making the chances of you having a school shooting at your school very slim. But some want to end all school shootings, which I understand.

Since we can't legislate evil, and stop all killers from taking innocent lives, we must harden our targets. So, if you want to stop ALL school shootings, here is what you must do—Your schools must look like an airport, a courthouse, or the Whitehouse. Believe me when I tell you, politicians and government legislators know how to keep people safe. They walk through security every day as they enter their building and walk into meetings. Government officials know how to keep your kids safe, they just don't want to spend the money it would take to accomplish that goal. Imagine every school in America equipped like an airport or courthouse.... body scanners, X-ray machines, multiple TSA type staff, multiple police officers, metal detectors, one or two K9's, and secured doors that set off an alarm when used by the wrong people, resulting in an arrest. Do you want to stop ALL school shootings? That is how you stop all school shootings. Your taxes will go up quite a bit to fund these secure buildings, and they would probably continue to increase to keep up with the fiscal needs for maintaining this level of security in schools.

So, will our government ever do this? I predict no, until a major massacre takes place, with hundreds of deaths, like the 9/11 attacks. Until that happens, in my opinion, no action will be taken by the government. And if 26 elementary school students shot to death doesn't get action from our government, nothing will be done until hundreds die, like the Kenya school attack. A more viable option would be to join multiple schools together into one school, and have it in a very secure building, much like an airport. The last option, and probably a good choice for many parents, is to homeschool their children, and have them learn on computers in the comfort and safety of their own homes.

As I examine school massacres over the years, I have closely watched the details of each school massacre, the death toll, the number of injured, and the method of murder carried out. The weapon used can make the shooting deadlier, but there is no guarantee. As I already stated, time and easy access to victims makes a shooting deadly. As you examine the deadliest school shootings and mass murders in our country, at the time of the writing of this book, you will notice the Vegas had Massacre has 58 deaths, the Pulse nightclub in Orlando had 49 deaths, and Virginia Tech has 32 deaths. At Vegas and Orlando, the gunman used a rifle, while the Virginia Tech killer used two small handguns. I also closely examined the recent massacres in Sandy Hook with 26 deaths, and Parkland with 17 deaths. And you can't forget Columbine with 13 deaths. What is the connection? Some used handguns, some used shotguns, and some used rifles. But in all these shootings, the gunman had plenty of time to carry out his massacre, and in each of these incidents, he had easy access to victims.

The Vegas gunman had a long time to carry out his shooting, possibly thirty minutes or more, and the Pulse nightclub killer had approximately fifteen minutes, or more. The Virginia Tech killer had fifteen minutes, and the Parkland killer had eleven minutes. The Columbine killers had nearly an hour. As far as access to victims, all these incidents proved the shooters had easy access to their victims, with classroom doors unlocked in Virginia Tech, Sandy Hook, Sante Fe, Texas and Columbine. In Parkland, students were either stranded in the hallway, or shot through classroom door windows. When given fifteen minutes, the Virginia Tech Killer killed thirty-two innocent students with two handguns. When law enforcement waits outside the school for eleven minutes and doesn't enter the building, you give the Parkland killer a chance to shoot thirty-four students, killing seventeen. But when police and first responders enter the crime scene quickly, the body count is always much lower. A recent school shooting in Great Falls, Maryland was ended in less than two minutes, and only one person was killed. The weapon used was a rifle, but since the gunman had little time and didn't have easy access to potential victims, the body count was nearly non-existent. A semi-automatic handgun is just as dangerous as a rifle, if the killer has time.

In the end, concerning school shootings, the biggest culprit, in my opinion, who should shoulder the greatest amount of blame, is the mainstream news media. Giving killers the fame they crave is complete nonsense, and should be illegal. This goes for all national news outlets, including CNN, Fox News, MSNBC, USA Today, Rolling Stone, People magazine, and all local news media outlets. When the Boston Marathon bomber killed innocent people in Massachusetts, Rolling Stone Magazine emblazoned their cover with his face, literally making him a rock star. While the media blitz drones day after day pertaining to the aforementioned events, the next school shooter and mass murderer is fantasizing about his or her murder spree, and dreaming about one day being the focus on the national news. The national and local news media is literally putting out a casting call for the next school shooter. And guess who is watching? Another lonely disturbed, suicidal psychopath, who wants to get even with his abusers, become famous, and hopefully die in the process. As Cruz tweeted before his attack, "I want to be a professional school shooter."

Can we make it illegal for the mainstream news media to make these killers stars? Absolutely, positively yes. Many other countries have laws and don't allow the news media to profit off of juvenile murder cases. For example, Canada is one who doesn't allow a teen killer to be named on news media, at any level. There have been a few deadly school shootings in Canada, but most if not all citizens of the United States cannot name one Canadian school shooter, or mass murderer, because they don't know who they are. Just imagine how many school shootings and mass murders we might prevent if we refused to glorify killers? This is something to think about and talk to our congressmen and congresswomen about.

Until the government decides to act and equip our schools like airports, we will have to be diligent and proactive and do everything we can do to keep our students, staff and administrators safe. I will share with you something I share with my live audiences, and I call it the "Five D's of School Safety." These gems are from police trainer and good friend Lt Col Dave Grossman, who also writes crucially important books in this genre. Maybe you can pick up a few tips from this list, make some changes and do your part in making your school the safest place it can be during school hours.

DENIAL

The first "D" is Denial, and many of our schools are still in denial, thinking it can't happen at their school or in their community. Other venues like churches, malls and movie theaters can also be in denial. You can't make any progress towards a safer school when your leadership and staff is in denial. How do you overcome that? You can invite them to a realistic training, by speakers and trainers like myself or Col. Dave Grossman. How can you tell if you've succeeded in getting your school or organization out of denial? You won't hear the phrase "it won't happen here" anymore. You will notice a budget increase in safety, the hiring of law enforcement, active shooter drills, and the investment in hardware and software that helps make the building or business a safer place.

DETECT

The second "D" is Detect, and you must get good at detecting potential threats from your student body. I would recommend an anonymous tip line, along with fake social media accounts to track your students' posts and activities. You should also educate everyone in your building, your teachers, staff, administration, bus drivers, kitchen staff, and custodians. I would also recommend a school assembly that allows you to teach and train the students on what to look for, since they stop most school attacks. Other ideas might be random searches by police K9, both inside the school, as well as the parking lot. Continue to preach to the student body and staff, "If you see something, say something." My school assembly curriculum is now available now available in my website store.

DETER

The third D is Deter, and the best deterrent to an active shooter or someone wanting to inflict harm on your school, church or mall would be an armed police officer. Most violent attackers don't want to encounter anyone with a gun, especially a trained member of law enforcement, so they will likely strike at a location with no sign of armed resistance. Places where large groups of people gather, with no guns allowed, called gun free zones, are what I call "soft targets," and the ideal place for a massacre. Remember, unarmed security is not a deterrent, but more so "crowd control" to stop petty crimes and to call the police when something serious happens. I recommend that your armed law enforcement officers are visible, and their marked police cars should be parked out front as an added visual deterrent. Lastly, part of the deter process is to lock your exterior doors, and place bullet resistant tint on the windows, all to slow a killer down as he or she attempts to shoot through glass doors and windows. One brand of bullet restraint window tint can be found at ArmouredOne.com.

Finally, when I get asked the controversial question about arming teachers, here is my typical response. If you can place armed law enforcement officers in your schools, that is the best option. And if you have police departments close by, who can respond in three to five minutes, you probably don't need to arm your teachers. I also fear that if a shooting were to happen in your school, and police officers were coming in quickly to end the shooting and kill the attacker, they might mistake the language arts teacher holding a gun for the killer, and an unnecessary tragedy might take place with the armed teacher shot and killed. But, if the police are far away, and it would take them fifteen to thirty minutes or more to respond to a shooting at your school, then you might consider arming a few staff members with concealed weapons. Those staff members would have to attend a rigorous training class during the summer, like a police academy. And you must trust those teachers to act accordingly during a dangerous incident. Arming teachers or other staff members is a highly controversial practice and of course, is contingent upon school board policy for each district that considers this method as an alternative or addition to other school safety measures.

Please remember, the most dangerous hour of the school day is the first hour, when most school attacks take place. Other times that can be dangerous is anytime students are gathered, including lunch hours, sporting events and school assemblies. The bottom line: Armed police officers stop school shootings, and very few attacks and massacres take place where there is an armed school resource officer.

DELAY

The fourth "D" is Delay, and once you have an active shooter in your school or building, trying to kill innocent students and staff, it is imperative to slow them down until the police can arrive. Keep in mind it may take police five, ten or fifteen minutes to respond, so you will have to slow this killer down until they arrive. Most active shooter situations are over within six minutes, so you may need to protect those under your watch for at least six minutes. How do you do that?

In a school setting, interior classroom doors must always be locked during the day. This means for each class period or hour. This is a cheap, no nonsense way to aid in ensuring student and staff safety. Basically, you are in lockdown every hour or period. Along with classroom doors being locked, you should have safe glass that can't be easily broken or shot out by an intruder. You want to make sure a gunman can't break the glass of a classroom door and open the door handle from the inside. You should practice lockdown or active shooter drills, whether you have a member of law enforcement in your building or not. Knowing the response time and the average length of a shooting incident, the first responders most likely are students, school staff, and administration. Also remember, Nikolas Cruz in Parkland killed most of his victims by shooting through the windows of classroom doors.

DEFEAT

The fifth "D" is Defeat, and this is more for law enforcement and security personnel. To defeat an active killer, you must enter the building or school as quickly as you can to let the active shooter know you have arrived. Hitting your siren on your vehicle as you pull in is a great way to instill fear and panic in the killer, and it may speed up his or her suicide. Also announce "police" as you enter, again, to instill panic and fear in the shooter, in hopes that he will stop killing innocent teachers and students. Now the shooter must decide to either flee the building or end his or her own life. The rule here is to enter the building or school as quickly as you can to reduce casualties. Time is crucial.... it's as simple as that. When law enforcement delays entry to a building, like Columbine, Virginia Tech and Parkland, many students die.

Other ideas to assist law enforcement in defeating the mass killer includes providing law enforcement gun safes to store rifles and long guns in the building. This helps so law enforcement doesn't have to run to their vehicles to retrieve weapons. Cameras that are monitored are always a positive addition to a school safety plan and can be helpful to monitor the killer's whereabouts and provide police and staff with an update over the speaker system. Remember, some camera systems are on a delay, which confused law enforcement and school administration in Parkland, Florida. This delays police and medical response time to help injured students.

CHAPTER EIGHT
THE INTERVENTION

Helping a potential teen killer or school shooter is not an easy task. Once they have multiple causes, they are in the danger zone and in need of intervention. As they begin displaying warning signs, someone needs to not only recognize these signs, but get the person displaying these troubling signs help. The problem is most unstable teens are living and growing up in unstable homes, being raised by unstable parents. That becomes a real challenge, trying to "save" a kid who must go back to and survive in a dysfunctional home every night. That being said, these are the things we can do to help a potentially violent juvenile before they choose to kill.

It goes without saying that we must do what we can to eliminate the causes I talk about in my books and live trainings. Let's touch on each one. First, you need to make sure the teen you are trying to help is living in a stable environment, both in school and at home, free from physical, sexual and mental abuse. This may be your biggest challenge, but it is, by far, the most important step. Make sure this person is not experiencing bullying at school and find out if it's been reported to school staff by talking to a counselor or principal. Of course, asking the student themselves should be done first, and following up with school staff to verify the information given to you by the student.

A very important piece of every young person's life is a father. Does this person have a healthy, loving father? If not, they need a positive male role model, be it a grandfather, uncle, coach or a Big Brother volunteer. Another possible negative effect is violent media, including violent movies, music, video games, television and pornography. Is someone monitoring this child's devices to see if they are flooding their adolescent brains with death, destruction, murder, sodomy, torture and rape? Is this child displaying an interest in deadly weapons, including guns, knives, bombs, and explosives? They should not have access to deadly weapons, to prevent a possible homicide or suicide.

Does this person have any suicidal thoughts and ideologies? Are they displaying any warning signs of suicide or self-abuse? Make sure you know the signs of suicide and keep a close eye on their possible cries for help. Is this person on any drugs, illegal or prescribed? Are they abusing alcohol? This could alter their thinking, make them depressed, and could lead to a tragedy. Could this young person be in a gang or cult? Are they posting anything strange on social media, or dressing differently? Are they hanging with new friends? I would also make sure their friends, boyfriends and girlfriends are good and positive influences, and not negative influences.

Is this young person living in poverty? Are they in need of the necessities of life, like food, clothing, and school supplies? Any help you could give them would eliminate this cause and make their life much more tolerable. Is someone implanting some positive, spiritual morals and beliefs into this person? These young people need someone to give them hope when they go through a hard time. Does this person have any structure in their life, a sense of normality? If not, do your part to bring some structure and routine to their life. And last but not least, are there any signs of mental illness? If so, are they being treated for their mental health issues? Many of our teens who are struggling with mental illness go untreated, so seeking professional help and possible medication could be a game changer for this person.

Maybe the person you are trying to help needs to get away from their current situation, their current friends, and possibly their unstable family structure, and enter a therapeutic school. There are plenty of schools nationwide where juveniles who are expressing violent tendencies or a sexual deviance can go and attend school, take advantage of intense therapy and counseling, and live in a lock-up facility where they can't hurt anyone else or themselves.

If you see the warning signs of possible violence, you must alert everyone surrounding this juvenile, and everyone who meets them. This includes the parents or guardians, school administrators, counselors, teachers, police officers, youth pastors, and anyone else who might be in danger.

The following is what I call my "Eight R's of Juvenile Homicide Prevention." If we can take these important steps, we might stop some teen killers and school shooters, and get them help before it is too late.

1. REPORT bullying-This is the number one cause of both school shootings and teen suicide.
2. REMOVE children from abusive homes-CPS needs to take abuse cases seriously and investigate and remove children from those situations if abuse is occurring.
3. RESTRICT the sale of violent entertainment to children-I think there needs to be laws to protect children from violent and pornographic teen entertainment, the same way we protect children from purchasing pornography.
4. REGULATE substance abuse and underage drinking-We need to continue to be diligent regarding drug and alcohol abuse and continue to support the DARE program and other school and community initiatives to counter substance abuse.
5. REQUEST more gang prevention programs from your community-Gangs are responsible for most of the murders in this country, so gang prevention programs, community programs, and job opportunities for children of an employable age is vital to prevent gang involvement.
6. REQUIRE gun owners to secure their weapons in steel safes-If we can get gun owners to lock up their weapons in steel safes, we could prevent thousands of teen murders, and many if not most school shootings. I think there should be a law enacted, for those possessing firearms, that you are legally responsible to

lock them up in a steel safe. This is the kind of "gun control" that would work.

7. RETURN to spiritual involvement, church attendance, and the discipline of children-When we took prayer out of schools, and families stopped attending church on Sundays, we began a downward slide to where we are today. The violence and pornography that is accepted in this country today would have never been accepted back in the 1940's and 1950's, and even in more recent times. Although I don't see us as a society returning to that level of spirituality, families can involve children in activities to help them develop faith and have some kind of spiritual belief to lean on throughout their lives.

8. RELOCATE to a safer neighborhood and school system-I know there are times when poverty is so pervasive, that many can't move out of a gang-ridden or dangerous neighborhood. But this is very important if you want your children to stay away from gangs and street crime. Move to a suburb, even if you must rent a small apartment. My family did this, and at times, I have done the same. When your children begin heading toward trouble or the wrong crowd, move them to a new, safer environment. That is your responsibility as a parent.

THE MILLENNIALS

Our young generation is unlike any generation we have ever seen. They demand you think like them, and if you don't agree with them, they will accuse you of hate. They are quick to throw around the terms of racism, sexism, bigotry and homophobia against those who disagree with them. There are several reasons for these actions, and I will try to explain them as best as I can. And remember, this doesn't apply to every young person today, but is a general description of this generation and many of the young people born in the last twenty years.

For starters, Millennials were raised with the wrong parenting strategies. They were told they were all winners, and they could be whatever they wanted to be. They were given medals and trophies for finishing last, the same trophy as the winner of the game or tournament. They were not disciplined growing up and got away with bad behavior. Their families also strayed from spiritual activities and church, so they were not raised with a spiritual and faith-based upbringing. In the real world, we are not all winners, and we don't always win. We also don't always date or marry the person we would like to marry, and we don't always get the job we want or the promotion we think we deserve. I personally don't always win, but I also never lose. I either win or learn, but that is another story for another time.

This current generation of young people were raised on technology and spend an ungodly amount of time in front of a screen. Computers, cell phones, video games, and television dictate their days and evenings. They spend more time in front of the screen and little time going out with real friends. Most of their friends are on social media and might not be people they will ever meet face-to-face. They date online, with apps like Tinder, and they have sex online with internet porn, which allows them to watch free sex videos all day long. Their inability to interact with actual people is diminished or never fully developed. When they venture out into the real world to work and play, they struggle with interactions and daily tasks like work and relationships. They have few coping skills and low self-esteem.

Add the above-mentioned issues into broken family dynamics, and the Disney-Daddy problem further compounds the issue. Children bounce back and forth between homes, from Mom and her new partner's home to Dad and his new partner's home. Both couples are trying to be the "favorite" by giving their kids whatever they want and skipping discipline. This is the problem with divorce, and one of its negative effects on children. Today, many parents want to be their children's friends and not their parents. Kids need parents, not more friends. Don't give your children everything they want, but instead teach them values and the meaning of hard work. Discipline them when they need it. You may not be the most popular parent, but someday, they will understand that you loved them and did the right thing.

Ultimately, this is the reason for the high opioid, crack and meth problems, and the countless stories of young people throwing their lives away. The suicide rate is the highest it has ever been, and according to the CDC from 2007 to 2015, the suicide rate for teen females rose 50%. For teen males suicide rates climbed 30%. Our young people are killing themselves with drugs and suicide. Along with their apparent self-destruction, they are killing each other. Teens kill five people every day, and this decade has been the deadliest school shooting decade ever.

So, parents, I implore you to teach your children that they will not always win. Encourage them to unplug from technology and get out and experience life. Encourage your children to get involved in sports, clubs, and hobbies, and to interact with real, live people. Teach them morals and values and encourage faith-based activities like church. Teach your children to work for nice things, instead of giving them everything. And lastly, when discipline is needed, please discipline your children so they experience boundaries and consequences. As the bible says in Proverbs 22:6, "Train up a child in the way he or she should go; even when they are old, they will not depart from it."

CHAPTER NINE
DON'T BE A VICTIM-
THE CRIME PREVENTION PIECE

HOME SAFETY

After interviewing hundreds of killers throughout my career, at the end of the interviews, I always ask the perpetrators about crime prevention and what they wouldn't want to encounter while committing crimes. I ask them, "If you were coming to my home tonight to victimize my family, what would you not want to see?" They typically respond with three answers in various descriptions. Dog, gun, and security system-in that order. After doing this for over thirty years, I strongly feel that if you want to be safe in your home you need at least two of three deterrents. So, if you are comfortable with a gun and own one, I would recommend you have a security system or a dog. If you are not comfortable with guns, you must own a dog and a security system. You must own two of the three, and remember, one is not enough.

Dog: Killers and bad guys don't want to see a dog in your home, as this is the number one deterrent. They do not like dogs for numerous reasons, both the danger of being bitten and the possibility of being detected when the dog barks, alerting the homeowner. When I speak to people who don't like or own guns, I tell them the good news, that a dog is more of a deterrent than a gun. And I don't mean a small dog,

I'm talking breeds such as; Rottweiler, Great Dane, German Shepard, Doberman, Boxer, or Pit Bull. These are deterrent dogs. Small dogs are not as much of a deterrent, even though they bark as well. And cats, well, they are just plain evil! Ok, just kidding, but your cat just might try to kill you in your sleep. On a serious note, cats are not a deterrent.

Gun: Killers and bad guys don't ever want to run into a gun, so yes, a gun is a deterrent. I am also aware a gun is not for everyone, so if you decide to use a gun as a piece of your crime prevention plan, you must take extra precautions. The best guns for self-protection are handguns, and for home protection you can also add a short shotgun. Three things are a must if you are going to own a gun: 1. You must be trained on gun safety. 2. You must keep your weapon in a locked, steel safe. 3. You must not use your weapon unless you feel your life is threatened. Displaying a weapon stops most of the dangerous encounters you may run into, but once you choose to pull the trigger, please make sure you feel your life is threatened, which justifies deadly force.

Security System: I feel the most effective security system is one that has recording cameras, as killers and bad guys tell me they will not mess with cameras, which assists in identifying them. There are numerous security system companies, some local, and some national. Names like ADT and SimpliSafe are common and cater to different needs. Adding cameras makes your system much more effective. I like the Nest home security cameras that you can purchase at Lowes and Home Depot. They usually run around $200, and once you download the app, you can monitor your home while you are away. Also, if someone would enter your home or yard, before the security system goes off, you will get a text that someone is in your home, and you can actually view the image on your phone or any device with Wi-Fi. It also sends me a text when it detects movement in the camera, letting me know if someone is walking outside of my home. It provides clear images in the dark, along with sound, and I can actually push a button and talk to the person in my home or yard. Last, make sure you have plenty of signage that people can see from the street or sidewalk, advertising that you have both a security system as well as cameras. You can find signs online that state "This home is under surveillance." Please make sure you add these signs to your security plan and place them by the street.

Along with the top three deterrents of home safety, here are a few more pieces of your security plan that I want to recommend. You need a safe home, or a safe room. If an incident happens at night, your master bedroom is your safe room, somewhat like the movie "Panic Room." Imagine you were trying to keep a killer out of your bedroom for ten to fifteen minutes until the police arrive, so you will need some good locks on your bedroom door. You should also charge your cell phone next to your bed so you can call for help, and you should have a handgun safe under your bed for quick access to your firearm should you choose to arm yourself.

Another aspect of safety and security is being invisible and not trackable. There are numerous websites that allow people to search for your information and location, and they include truepeoplesearch.com and pipl.com. How do you remain invisible to others who are trying to find your place of residence? Eliminate your home phone, own your home in an LLC, and receive your mail at a post office box or a UPS store mailbox. Never get mail or shipments to your home address.

You should also practice lockdown drills at home like children do at school, and practice how your family would respond to a possible threat or intruder. While the alarm is ringing, what are the members of your family going to do, and where are they going to be? Your kids need to hide in their locked bedroom and you, as the parent, may have a gun searching for the intruder. Have a plan so you don't get surprised if this really happens in your home. A person approached me at a training and told me a story about a friend in Michigan who heard an intruder in his home. As he exited his bedroom with a firearm, he noticed an intruder down the hallway of his home and opened fire, killing him. Unfortunately, two of the rounds missed the intruder, went through the dining room wall and killed his son sleeping in his bunk bed. It is a tragedy to say the least, when you kill the bad guy, and kill your only son. Have a plan to prevent a tragedy like this from happening in your home.

A final component of your plan should be to not allow strangers into your home for any reason. Your entire family needs to be on board with this, including your young children. For me, if I am going to allow a stranger into my home, which I don't do very often, I always have a concealed weapon on my person. This includes workers in my home, furniture delivery personnel, and people in other service businesses. If something cannot be delivered to your PO Box or UPS Store box, all deliveries should be left on your front door step. Try to limit the people you allow into your home. Every single time you have a stranger in your home, you open yourself and your loved ones up to the risk of something unfortunate happening at that time, or at a later time.

AUTOMOBILE SAFETY

Regarding being safe in your vehicle, if you use a GPS, never add your real home address to your GPS. Instead, use a local store or business near your home. We use a Walmart near our home as our home address, which is approximately five minutes away. I would also suggest you skip the window stickers telling people where you live, attend church, work, or where your kids attend school. Nobody needs to know that information. I would also recommend you not place stickers on your vehicle announcing that you have a cheerleader daughter and a wrestler son. Some serial killers like John Wayne Gacy liked wrestlers, and dangerous killers like Ed Kemper hunted for cheerleaders. The same would go for the stick figure family stickers, announcing how many children you have, and what gender they are.

TRAVEL SAFETY

When you travel and fly for business or pleasure, never tag your luggage with your name, phone number and address. The airline will tag your luggage and that is all they will need should they find it necessary to locate your bag.

LIVE IN CONDITION YELLOW

Condition yellow is always best described as being aware of your surroundings. It is also being prepared in the event something bad happens to you or near you. It is about being prepared, even though some would call it paranoid. I call this living in "condition yellow." Many people live in a state of "condition white," which is a condition where people are unaware of what is happening around them, thinking that bad things will more than likely not happen to them. These people really don't think about crime or violence, but unfortunately, crime and violence can visit us in any city, community, or small town. When you live in condition yellow and bad things happen, you can move to condition red, which is fight or survival mode. When you live in condition white and bad things happen, you usually move to condition black, which is shock mode. This is when people lay down and allow someone to kill them.

What does condition yellow look like? When I eat at a restaurant, I always place my back to the wall and face the door of the restaurant. I always keep a watchful eye on the entire restaurant, if something bad might happen. When I attend a movie, I sit in the back row of the theater, at the top of a stadium seating theater with a view of the entire theater and know where the exits are located. When I work out at the gym every morning, I carry a gym bag with a concealed weapon. When I bike ride, I have a bag under my seat which contains a handgun. I always try to be prepared, should something go wrong. You want to be ready if evil pays a visit to you, your family, or your location. When you walk into a room, an event, a class, or a meeting, always assess the room and decide what you would do if something bad should happen. Where would you run to, or where would you barricade yourself? Is there a locked room close by? Where are the exits? Also, check doors and windows to assess if they open and if they have locks.

CARRYING CONCEALED AND OFF DUTY

Concerning concealed weapons and self-defense, I have the luxury to be able to carry a concealed firearm pretty much wherever I go, so it is a very rare occurrence when I don't have a firearm near me or on my person. I am not a "gun nut," meaning I don't collect guns, I don't own hundreds of guns, and I don't shoot guns every weekend. I own a few different guns for protection, because I cannot afford armed security like politicians or celebrities. I would prefer to carry a police officer, but they are a bit too heavy to carry everywhere you go, so instead, I carry a concealed firearm. And I carry everywhere, including the gym, the swimming pool, on my bicycle, at church, at the beach, at the movies, and almost everywhere I go. People ask if I am paranoid, and my response is no. I am just being proactive and prepared. I hope I never need to use my weapons, but I have had to display it to people a time or two when I felt threatened. The only place I don't carry is Walt Disney World or Disneyland, but since I know they have plenty of armed security, I am comfortable not carrying at those amusement parks.

Regarding my law enforcement officers, I would encourage you to always carry off duty and never be caught without a weapon. The same could be said for those with concealed carry permits. If you are legally allowed to carry where you are going, I would encourage you to always carry. I am not a fan of open carry by the way, as I feel there is a bit of danger involved with that. I am a fan of concealed carry, and the only time people should know you have a gun on you is when shit has hit the fan and you feel your life is in danger. For civilians, if you are entering a place where weapons are not allowed, like a courthouse or Walt Disney World, make sure you have a secure place to store your weapon in the car, like a lockbox or gun safe. Be safe everyone, always keep your head on a swivel, be aware of your surroundings, and always be in condition yellow. Remember the saying, "Be polite, be humble and have a plan to kill everyone in the room."

CONCLUSION

I began this work in 1985, when I felt I could relate to troubled teens, since I came from a troubled home myself. Here I am, in 2019, still doing the very same thing nearly 35 years later. Like I tell teens, some of you have been dealt a good hand, and some have been dealt a bad hand. No matter what kind of hand you are dealt when playing your cards, you never fold, but play your cards to the fullest. The same goes for life. Some people have been dealt a good hand, meaning they came from good homes, have two parents that love them, grew up financially stable, and their homes were free from sexual, physical, or emotional abuse, as well as drug and alcohol abuse. If you have been dealt a good hand, you should immediately thank those who have raised you and praise them for providing you a good upbringing.

Unfortunately, others reading this can't say their upbringing was picturesque, and I am one of them. We were not raised by two stable parents who loved us, and our homes were not free from abuse and belittlement, nor were our homes free from substance abuse. We were not dealt a good hand, but we must play that hand. You must do everything you can to not only make it for yourself, but for those around you. You are not only playing this hand to better your life, but the lives that will follow you-your children and grandchildren. You are breaking the curse of instability and the chain of dysfunction. So, don't give up, play your hand to the fullest, make your pain your passion, and change the course of your family name and your lineage.

Once you turn your life around and you get control of your life, you can then begin to help others. You need to do your best to conquer your addictions, and change bad habits that have developed during your upbringing. Once you do this and you are stable and living a positive life, you then begin to reach out to others.

So how do we turn the tide of teen violence and the culture of death? How do we stop raising a generation of young killers? Here are a few ideas that I feel could make a difference and help stop this disturbing trend. I'm not sure we can really get anyone behind these ideas, but until we do, nothing will change. The first step is we need to stop celebrating killers and glamorizing their crimes. When a kid brings a gun to school and kills 17 people, he becomes an American celebrity, compliments of the mainstream news media, including CNN, Fox News, MSNBC, USA Today, People Magazine, Newsweek Magazine, Time Magazine, Rolling Stone Magazine, and hundreds of smaller, more localized television and newspaper outlets. These young killers know if they kill enough, and the right type of victims, they will become famous, household names, and many are seeking that. Let's sign a law that makes it illegal for the news media to mention the names of mass murderers, school shooters and serial killers, stripping them of the fame they crave. Instead, let's focus on the bravery of the first responder and let's celebrate the lives of the victims.

In our society and in our country, we no longer value human life. We want to focus on things like guns, laws, politics, and political organizations, but we, as a society, no longer value human life. We no longer respect others, and we no longer protect the dignity of others. We are always looking for a way to divide ourselves, instead to becoming one. It's all about the left or right, Republicans and Democrats, Conservatives and Liberals, Us vs Them. I watch news networks that have one goal and it is to talk negatively about the other party, or the current President, whoever that is. This needs to stop!

We raise our children immersed in violence, pornography, hate, perversion, and death. There is constant exposure to internet pornography, sick violent video games, disgusting torture films, violent and torture pornography, vile music, and non-stop violence and death on television and in movie theaters. Our children are raised on devices and WiFi, which is creating a generation of young people who have trouble relating to others outside of social media. The celebration of guns and death is rampant in this country, and we wonder why our kids are killing each other, instead of celebrating the good guys, who should always have the glory. As a culture we celebrate the bad guys. As our children are playing a murder simulation game for numerous hours every day, the same type of simulators we train our military and police with, these games constantly reinforce and reward children for killing others. There is constant repetition and positive affirmation of violence, death, murder, sex with prostitutes, strip clubs, street crime, and more. And we wonder!

There is hope...and it lies with you. Your efforts to be vigilant in watching not only your own children, but those in your extended family, neighborhood and community do pay off. If you watch for the warning signs, causes and triggers of teen violence, report the signs when you see them, and provide a positive, stable environment for your own children and those you love, we can save hundreds, if not thousands, in a combined effort of awareness and change to the culture we are living in. Be safe and message me if you need help.

Phil and Wendi Chalmers,
PhilChalmers.com

APPENDIX ONE
LONGEST LIST OF TEEN SCHOOL SHOOTINGS

This is a short and incomplete list of American school attacks carried out by teens, up to 19 years of age. They were purposeful killings, and not solely suicides or accidental killings. I didn't include gang and drive by shootings. Starting from most recent, I will include many of the 2017 and 2018 attacks, as well as some of the more deadly attacks in American history. And I don't count the suicide of the killer as a death number in these attacks.

The youngest school killer was a 6-year-old male in Flint, Michigan. The deadliest non-college/school attack by an active student is in Littleton, Colorado at 13 killed. The deadliest high school attacks by a non-active student was Newtown, Connecticut at 26 killed and Parkland, Florida at 17 killed. The deadliest college attack occurred in Blacksburg, Virginia with 32 killed, and the deadliest American school attack carried out by a person of any age is Bath Township, Michigan, which occurred on May 18, 1927. An angry adult blew up the school, killing multiple children and adults, and then killed himself. The death toll was 44 killed, 58 injured. The deadliest school massacre in the world occurred on September 1, 2004, in Beslan, Russia, where a group of extremists killed 334 children and adults, and injured another 783 more. The attackers were killed by Russian Special Forces. Also, please note that the number one cause of all school shootings is bullying.

10/29/18: Charlotte, North Carolina, 1 killed, 16 year old suspect, arrested

5/18/18: Santa Fe, Texas, 10 killed, 10 injured, 17 year old suspect, arrested

5/11/18: Palmdale, California, 1 injured, 14 year old suspect, arrested

4/20/18: Ocala, Florida, 1 injured, suspect arrested,

3/20/18: Great Mills, Maryland, 1 killed, 1 injured, 17 year old suspect, suicide

3/17/18: Birmingham, Alabama, 1 killed, 2 injured, 17 year old suspect, arrested

3/2/18: Mount Pleasant, Michigan, 2 killed, 19 year old suspect, arrested

2/14/18: Parkland, Florida, 17 killed, 17 injured, 19 year old suspect, arrested

2/1/18: Los Angeles, California, 2 injured, 12 year old female suspect, arrested

1/23/18: Benton, Kentucky, 2 killed, 18 injured, 15 year old suspect, arrested

9/20/17: Mattoon, Illinois, 1 injured, 14 year old suspect, arrested

9/13/17: Rockford, Washington, 1 killed, 3 injured, 15 year old suspect, arrested

1/20/17: West Liberty, Ohio, 1 injured, 17 year old suspect, arrested

10/25/16: Sandy, Utah, 1 injured, 14 year old suspect, arrested

10/11/16: Mobile, Alabama, 1 injured, 16 year old suspect, arrested

9/28/16: Townville, South Carolina, 2 killed, 2 injured, age unknown, arrested

9/9/16: Alpine, Texas, 1 killed, 2 injured, 14 year old female suspect, arrested

4/23/16: Antigo, Wisconsin, 1 killed, 2 injured, 16 year old suspect, killed by police

2/29/16: Middletown, Ohio, 4 injured, 14 year old suspect, arrested

2/12/16: Glendale, Arizona, 1 killed, 15 year old female suspect, suicide

10/9/15: Flagstaff, Arizona, 1 killed, 3 wounded, 18 year old suspect, arrested

9/30/15: Harrisburg, South Dakota, 1 injured, 16 year old suspect, arrested

5/12/15: Jacksonville, Florida, 2 injured, 16 year old suspect, arrested

12/12/14: Portland, Oregon, 4 injured, 18 year old suspect, arrested

10/24/14: Marysville, Washington, 4 killed, 3 injured, 15 year old suspect, suicide

10/3/14: Fairburn, Georgia, 1 killed, 18 year old suspect, arrested

9/30/14: Louisville, Kentucky, 1 injured, 15 year old suspect, arrested

6/10/14: Troutdale, Oregon, 2 killed, 1 injured, 15 year old suspect, suicide

2/10/14: Salisbury, North Carolina, 1 injured, 17 year old suspect, arrested

1/27/14: Carbondale, Illinois, 1 injured, 18 year old suspect, arrested

1/24/14: Orangeburg, South Carolina, 1 killed, 19 year old suspect, arrested

1/17/14: Philadelphia, Pennsylvania, 2 injured, 17 year old suspect, arrested

1/14/14: Roswell, New Mexico, 2 injured, 12 year old suspect, arrested

12/12/13: Centennial, Colorado, 1 killed, 18 year old suspect, suicide

10/21/13: Sparks, Nevada, 2 killed, 2 injured, 12 year old suspect, suicide

1/10/13: Taft, California, 2 injured, 16 year old suspect, arrested

8/27/12: Perry Hall, Maryland, 1 injured, 15 year old suspect, arrested

2/27/12: Chardon, Ohio, 3 killed, 3 injured, 17 year old suspect, arrested

10/24/11: Fayetteville, North Carolina, 1 injured, 15 year old suspect, arrested

5/23/11: Pearl City, Hawaii, 1 injured, 14 year old suspect, arrested

3/25/11: Martinsville, Indiana, 1 injured, arrested

1/5/11: Omaha, Nebraska, 1 killed, 2 injured, 18 year old suspect, suicide

2/5/10: Madison, Alabama, 1 killed, 14 year old suspect, arrested

11/13/08: Fort Lauderdale, Florida, 1 killed, 15 year old suspect, arrested

8/21/08: Knoxville, Tennessee, 1 killed, 15 year old suspect, arrested

2/12/08: Oxnard, California, 1 killed, 14 year old suspect, arrested

2/11/08: Memphis, Tennessee, 1 injured, 17 year old suspect, arrested

2/4/08: Memphis, Tennessee, 1 injured, 16 year old suspect, arrested

10/10/07: Cleveland, Ohio, 4 injured, 14 year old suspect, suicide

3/7/07: Compton, California, 1 injured, 17 year old suspect, arrested

1/3/07: Tacoma, Washington, 1 killed, 18 year old suspect, arrested

9/29/06: Cazenovia, Wisconsin, 1 killed, 15 year old suspect, arrested

8/30/06: Hillsborough, North Carolina, 2 injured, 17 year old suspect, arrested

3/14/06: Reno, Nevada, 2 injured, 14 year old suspect, arrested

2/23/06: Roseburg, Oregon, 1 injured, 14 year old suspect, arrested

11/8/05: Jacksboro, Tennessee, 1 killed, 2 injured, 15 year old suspect, arrested

9/13/05: Chicago, Illinois, 1 injured, 15 year old suspect, arrested

3/21/05: Red Lake, Minnesota, 7 killed, 5 injured, 16 year old suspect, suicide

3/2/05: Dover, Tennessee, 1 killed, 14 year old suspect, arrested

5/7/04: Randallstown, Maryland, 4 injured, 18 year old suspect, arrested

2/9/04: East Greenbush, New York, 1 injured, 16 year old suspect, arrested

9/24/03: Cold Spring, Minnesota, 2 killed, 15 year old suspect, arrested

4/24/03: Red Lion, Pennsylvania, 1 killed, 14 year old suspect, suicide

4/14/03: New Orleans, Louisiana, 1 killed, 3 wounded, 18 and 17 year old suspects, arrested

10/29/02: Jersey City, New Jersey, 1 wounded, 15 year old suspect, arrested

1/15/02: New York City, New York, 2 wounded, 17 year old student, arrested

3/30/01: Gary, Indiana, 1 killed, 17 year old suspect, arrested

3/22/01: El Cajon, California, 5 injured, 18 year old suspect, arrested

3/7/01: Williamsport, Pennsylvania, 1 injured, 14 year old student, arrested

3/5/01: Santee, California, 2 killed, 13 injured, 15 year old suspect, arrested

2/23/01: Isla Vista, California, 4 killed, 1 injured, 18 year old suspect, arrested

9/26/00: New Orleans, Louisiana, 2 injured, 13 year old suspects, arrested

5/26/00: Lake Worth, Florida, 1 killed, 13 year old suspect, arrested

2/29/00: Flint, Michigan, 1 killed, 6 year old suspect, arrested

12/6/99: Fort Gibson, Oklahoma, 6 injured, 13 year old suspect, arrested

11/19/99: Deming, New Mexico, 1 killed, 13 year old suspect, arrested

5/20/99: Conyers, Georgia, 6 injured, 15 year old suspect, arrested

4/20/99: Littleton, Colorado, 13 killed, 21 injured, 17 and 18 year old suspects, suicide

1/8/99: Carrollton, Georgia, 1 killed, 17 year old suspect, arrested

6/15/98: Richmond, Virginia, 2 killed, 14 year old suspect, arrested

5/21/98: Springfield, Oregon, 2 killed, 25 injured, 15 year old suspect, arrested

5/19/98: Fayetteville, Tennessee, 1 killed, 18 year old suspect, arrested

4/24/98: Edinboro, Pennsylvania, 1 killed, 3 injured, 14 year old suspect, arrested

3/24/98: Jonesboro, Arkansas, 5 killed, 10 injured, 11 and 13 years old, arrested and released

12/15/97: Stamps, Arkansas, 14 year old suspect, 2 injured, arrested

12/1/97: West Paducah, Kentucky, 3 killed, 5 injured, 14 year old suspect, arrested

10/15/97: Palmetto, Florida, 1 injured, 13 year old suspect, arrested

10/1/97: Pearl, Mississippi, 2 killed, 7 injured, 16 year old suspect, arrested

2/19/97: Bethel, Alaska, 2 killed, 2 injured, 16 year old suspect, arrested

1/27/97: West Palm Beach, Florida, 1 killed, 14 year old suspect, arrested

10/9/96: Sherwood, Arkansas, 1 killed, 14 year old suspect, arrested

9/25/96: Decatur, Georgia, 1 killed, 2 injured, 16 year old suspect, arrested

9/17/96: State College, Pennsylvania, 1 killed, 2 injured, 19 year old suspect, arrested

2/2/96: Moses Lake, Washington, 3 killed, 1 injured, 14 year old suspect, arrested

1/19/96: Washington, D.C., 1 killed, 16 year old suspect, arrested

11/15/95: Lynnville, Tennessee, 2 killed, 1 injured, 17 year old suspect, arrested

10/12/95: Blackville, South Carolina, 1 killed, 1 injured, 16 year old suspect, suicide

9/29/95: Tavares, Florida, 1 killed, 14 year old suspect, arrested

1/12/95: Seattle, Washington, 2 injured, 15 year old suspect, arrested

10/12/94: Greensboro, North Carolina, 1 injured, 16 year old suspect, suicide

4/21/94: Nashville, Tennessee, 1 killed, 14 year old suspect, arrested

4/12/94: Butte, Montana, 1 killed, 10 year old suspect, arrested

1/24/94: Columbia, South Carolina, 1 killed, 16 year old suspect, arrested

5/24/93: Pennsburg, Pennsylvania, 1 killed, 15 year old suspect, arrested

5/14/93: Irving, Texas, 1 killed, 17 year old suspect, arrested

2/22/93: Los Angeles, California, 1 killed, 15 year old suspect, arrested

1/18/93: Grayson, Kentucky, 2 killed, 17 year old suspect, arrested

12/14/92: Great Barrington, Massachusetts, 2 killed, 4 injured, 18 year old suspect, arrested

3/5/92: Obetz, Ohio, 1 injured, 13 year old suspect, arrested

2/26/92: Brooklyn, New York, 2 killed, 15 year old suspect, arrested

9/18/91: Crosby, Texas, 1 killed, 15 year old suspect, arrested

12/5/89: McKeesport, Pennsylvania, 1 injured, 16 year old suspect, suicide

12/16/88: Virginia Beach, Virginia, 1 killed, 1 injured, arrested

11/22/88: Abilene, Texas, 1 injured, 16 year old suspect, arrested

9/26/88: Greenwood, South Carolina, 2 killed, 9 injured, 19 year old suspect, arrested

2/11/88: Largo, Florida, 1 killed, 2 injured, arrested

9/28/87: Lansing, Illinois, 1 injured, 16 year old suspect, arrested

4/16/87: Detroit, Michigan, 1 killed, 2 injured, 14 year old suspect, arrested

3/2/87: DeKalb, Missouri, 1 killed, 12 year old suspect, suicide

12/4/86: Lewistown, Montana, 14 year old suspect, 1 killed, 3 injured, arrested

5/9/86: Fayetteville, North Carolina, 3 injured, 17 year old suspect, arrested

4/29/86: Senath, Missouri, 1 killed, 16 year old suspect, arrested

3/6/86: Dolton, Illinois, 1 injured, 14 year old suspect, arrested

12/10/85: Portland, Connecticut, 1 killed, 2 injured, 13 year old suspect, arrested

11/27/85: Spanaway, Washington, 2 killed, 14 year old suspect, suicide

10/18/85, Detroit, Michigan, 6 injured, 16 year old suspect, arrested

1/21/85: Goddard, Kansas, 1 killed, 3 injured, 14 year old suspect, arrested

5/17/84: Pleasant Hill, Iowa, 1 killed, 17 year old suspect, suicide

1/20/83: St Louis, Missouri, 1 killed, 1 injured, 13 year old suspect, suicide

11/12/82: Jackson, Mississippi, 1 killed, 18 year old suspect, suicide

4/7/82: Littleton, Colorado, 1 killed, 14 year old suspect, arrested

3/19/82: Las Vegas, Nevada, 1 killed, 2 injured, 17 year old suspect, arrested

10/31/80: Hueytown, Alabama, 1 injured, 17 year old suspect, suicide

1/7/80: Stamps, Arkansas, 1 killed, 16 year old suspect, arrested

1/29/79: San Diego, California, 2 killed, 9 injured, 16 year old female suspect, arrested

10/17/78: Lanett, Alabama, 1 injured, 13 year old suspect, arrested

10/17/78: University City, Missouri, 4 injured, 18 year old suspect, arrested

5/18/78: Austin, Texas, 1 killed, 13 year old suspect, arrested

2/22/78: Lansing, Michigan, 1 killed, 1 injured, 15 year old suspect, arrested

2/9/78: St Albans, West Virginia, 1 killed, 14 year old suspect, arrested

4/7/77: Whitharral, Texas, 1 killed, 17 year old suspect, arrested

2/12/76: Detroit, Michigan, 5 injured, 15 year old suspect, arrested

9/11/75: Oklahoma City, Oklahoma, 1 killed, 5 injured, 16 year old suspect, arrested

12/30/74: Olean, New York, 3 killed, 11 injured, 18 year old suspect, arrested and suicide

3/22/74: Brownstown, Indiana, 1 killed, 17 year old suspect, arrested

1/17/74: Chicago, Illinois, 1 killed, 14 year old suspect, arrested

2/2/71: Philadelphia, Pennsylvania, 1 killed, 14 year old suspect, arrested

11/20/70: Detroit, Michigan, 1 injured, 15 year old suspect, arrested

11/19/69: Tomah, Wisconsin, 1 killed, 14 year old suspect, arrested

1/23/69: Washington, D.C., 1 killed, 18 year old suspect, arrested

5/22/68: Miami, Florida, 2 injured, 15 year old suspect, arrested

3/25/68: High Point, North Carolina, 1 killed, 15 year old suspect, arrested

5/3/67: Northlake, Illinois, 1 killed, 1 injured, 18 year old suspect, arrested

11/12/66: Mesa, Arizona, 5 killed, 2 injured, 18 year old suspect, arrested

10/5/66: Grand Rapids, Minnesota, 1 killed, 1 injured, 15 year old suspect, arrested

4/27/66: Bay Shore, New York, 1 killed, 16 year old suspect, arrested
10/17/61: Denver, Colorado, 1 killed, 1 injured, 14 year old suspect, arrested
3/30/60: Alice, Texas, 1 killed, 14 year old suspect, arrested
5/1/58: Massapequa, New York, 1 killed, 15 year old suspect, arrested
3/4/58: Brooklyn, New York, 1 injured, 17 year old suspect, arrested
10/2/57: New York, New York, 1 injured, 15 year old suspect, arrested
5/4/56: Seat Pleasant, Maryland, 1 killed, 2 injured, 15 year old suspect, arrested
4/9/52: New York, New York, 1 killed, 15 year old suspect, arrested
3/12/51: Union Mills, North Carolina, 2 killed, 16 and 19 year old suspects, arrested
7/22/50: New York, New York, 1 injured, 16 year old suspect, arrested
6/25/46: Brooklyn, New York, 1 injured, 16 year old suspect, arrested
10/2/42: New York, New York, 1 killed, 14 year old suspect, arrested
9/24/37: Toledo, Ohio, 1 injured, 12 year old suspect, arrested
3/4/1920: Cincinnati, Ohio, 1 injured, 14-year-old suspect, arrested
2/14/1920: Durant, Oklahoma, 1 injured, 15-year-old suspect, arrested
4/6/1904: Chicago, Illinois, 1 killed, 16-year-old suspect, arrested
7/21/1903: Jackson, Kentucky, 2 killed, 1 injured, 15-year-old suspect, killed

ADDITIONAL DATA

The first school attack in American history: July 26, 1764, in Greencastle, Pennsylvania, 10 killed, 2 injured, Enoch Brown School Massacre, occurred during the Pontiac War. Carried out by four American Indians, they shot and killed the schoolmaster and nine children, killing the children with knives and hatchets.

The deadliest American school attack occurred at Virginia Tech College, with 32 people killed, including the gunman. The deadliest high school attack by an active student remains Columbine, with 13 killed and dozens injured.

The youngest school shooting perpetrator is 6-year-old Dedrick

Owens, who fatally shot 6 year- old Kayla Rolland at Buell Elementary School in Flint, Michigan.

School attacks by decade:

1800's: 36 attacks, with the deadliest involving six killed
1900 to 1950: 62 attacks, with the deadliest involving five killed
1951 to 1959: 16 attacks, with the deadliest involving two killed
1960 to 1969: 18 attacks, with the deadliest involving seventeen killed
1970-1979: 30 attacks, with the deadliest involving seven killed
1980-1989: 39 attacks, with the deadliest involving three killed
1990-1999: 62 attacks, with the deadliest involving fifteen killed
2000-2009: 62 attacks, with the deadliest involving thirty three killed
2010-2019: 149 attacks, with the deadliest involving 28 killed

This list includes high schools and colleges, and the killers could be adults as well as teens. The number killed also includes the killer if they chose suicide.

APPENDIX TWO
HELPFUL WEBSITES

PHILCHALMERS.COM-The author's website, where you can download media kits, email the author, and locate his social media pages.

AFSP.ORG-American Foundation for Suicide Prevention.

AZLYRICS.COM-Read the lyrics to just about every song released in America.

BOLOSTICK.COM-Affordable door barricade device

BULLYCIDE.ORG-Help with the bullying problem, and about the connection between bullying and suicide. Driven by mothers.

COMMONSENSEMEDIA.ORG-Media review website including articles for parents.

COVENANTEYES.COM-Help with porn addiction.

CRIMESIDER.COM-Crime headlines, by CBS News.

CRIMEWATCHDAILY.COM-Daily crime headlines.

CURIOSITYANDHEROIN.ORG-Help for heroin addiction

DARE.ORG-Drug Abuse Resistance Education program for schools

INHALANTS.ORG-Inhalant abuse information.

JASONFOUNDATION.COM-Help with the prevention of youth suicide.

KILLOLOGY.COM-National speaker and award-winning author Col Dave Grossman's website. His training compliments my training very well, and both of us are invited to many national and state law enforcement conferences.

METHPROJECT.ORG-Before and after photos of meth users, with useful educational advertisements.

MYMOBILEWATCHDOG.COM and MSPY.COM: Cell phone and computer monitoring system.

NASRO.ORG-National Association of School Resource Officers.

NATSAP.ORG-The National Association of Therapeutic Schools, which has a list of nine-month lockdown facilities nationwide.

NOBULLY.ORG-Bullying definition with programs for schools and communities.

OHHLA.COM-The Original Hip Hop Lyric Archive, where you can find the lyrics for nearly every rap song.

PARENTALGUIDE.ORG-A media guide for parents of all media

PLUGGEDIN.COM-Music, Movie and Video Game reviews from a Christian perspective. My favorite media review site.

PROTECTYOUNGEYES.COM-Another great website for help with social media and phone apps.

RAPTORTECH.COM-School visitor management system

SAFESCHOOLS.COM-Help for schools with safety programs.

SCREENIT.COM-Movie review website

STREETDRUGS.ORG-Drug ID guides

SUICIDOLOGY.ORG-American Association of Suicidology.

TEEN-ANON.COM-Help with teen drug and alcohol addiction.

TEENINSTITUTE.ORG-Empowers teens to promote drug prevention.

TEENSAFE.COM-Cell phone and computer monitoring system.

THESOURCE4PARENTS.COM-Faith based website with help for parents and youth leaders.

THETVBOSS.ORG-Helps parents control television content, including the V chip.

TIP411.COM-Program for reporting threats anonymously.

ARMOUREDONE.COM-Window film that can make your glass smash resistant and bullet resistant.

TWLOHA.COM-To Write Love On Her Arms, provides help for cutting and self-abuse.

URBANDICTIONARY.COM-Great website for the teenager's lingo, as well as rap music lingo.

WORLDSTARHIPHOP.COM-I use this website for keeping up with youth culture, the rap music industry, and I also follow this website to keep up with the anti-police videos.

XXXCHURCH.COM-Help with porn addiction.

APPENDIX THREE
THE INTERVIEW

When you are called to interview a potentially violent teen, or you are tasked with interviewing the parents or guardians of a potentially dangerous teen, I recommend using this interview to determine if the teen exhibits any warning signs, causes and triggers of teen violence.

1. Has there been any trauma or abuse in this person's life, including physical abuse, sexual abuse, or mental abuse?
2. Has this person suffered any loss in their life, like the death of a parent or grandparent, the divorce of parents, or a breakup with a boyfriend or girlfriend?
3. Is this person being bullied at school, at home, or in their neighborhood?
4. Is this person experiencing domestic violence in their home?
5. Does this person have a father in their life? If not, does this person have a male role model in their home? Or life?
6. Is this person involved in the viewing of pornography of any kind? If so, what kind of pornography has been found? Is this person interested in violent pornography?
7. Does this person play violent video games, watch violent movies and videos, or listen to violent music?
8. Is this person fascinated with death? How do you know?
9. Are there any signs of suicide or depression? If so, what are the signs? Is there a family history of suicide? Have you noticed this person giving away any of their prized possessions recently?

10. Is this person using drugs or alcohol? If so, what kind?

11. Is this young person on any medications? If so, what kind, and what are the possible side effects?

12. Is it possible that this person might be involved in a gang or cult, like a street gang, white supremacy group, a satanic group, or a terrorist cell?

13. Is this person fascinated and/or obsessed with deadly weapons, like guns, knives, bombs, swords and hatchets? Are there guns in the home? Are they locked in a steel safe?

14. Does this person attend a church? Are they interested in spiritual based activities? Do they have a youth pastor?

15. Is this person disciplined when they don't follow the rules? How are they disciplined? What is their reaction, either by act and/or verbal statement?

16. Is this person wetting the bed? If so, how frequently?

17. Is this person fascinated with fire? Has this person ever set anything on fire?

18. Has this person ever harmed animals of any kind? If so, describe the animal and the act?

19. Has this person ever threatened to kill anyone? If so, who and how many times?

20. Does this person have a personal journal? Have you ever read it? Where is it located?

21. Have you ever found any violent or dark drawings, poetry, lyrics, or stories created by this person? Can you describe what it was, and where you found them?

22. Does this person have an online presence, like a website, blog or social media page? Have you ever looked at it? Is it Facebook, Instagram, Snapchat, or another social media platform?

23. Has this person ever showed any interest in other killers, like the Columbine school shooters, mass murderers, or serial killers? Can you describe the killer, and how you know there was an interest?

24. Does this person have any books with violent or dark ideologies, like the Satanic Bible, the Necronomicon, Mein Kampf?

25. Do they have any history of crime, like vandalism, shoplifting, domestic violence, physical assault, sexual assault, arson or running away?
26. Has this person ever partook in self-abuse, like cutting or burning themselves?
27. Is it possible that this person might be dating a much older person?
28. Are you concerned about any of their friends? If yes, can you describe why and who these friends are?
29. Do they spend a lot of time unsupervised either at home or at another location?
30. Have you ever caught this person peeping on another person, such as "peeping tom" activities on a neighbor? Have you ever caught this person peeping in on his mother, father, brother or sister?
31. Have you ever found strange items in their bedroom, like women's undergarments, a family member's undergarments, or other peculiar items, like women's jewelry?

If you would like author Phil Chalmers to assist you with the results of this questionnaire, please document the answers, and email them to PhilChalmersTV@gmail.com

APPENDIX FOUR
CONNECT WITH THE AUTHORS

Thank you so much for purchasing and reading this book and joining us in our fight to stop teen violence, make our schools safer, and save innocent children. There are several ways to connect with us, which will allow you to continue to be educated and keep up with what is new with us. We look forward to connecting with you, and hopefully meeting in person when we are on the road touring and presenting live trainings.

GET SOCIAL

Social media has been a great place for us to stay connected with our fans and to also continue to provide valuable information to the public. Here are the social media platforms we are currently using:
Facebook @TrueCrimePhil
Instagram @TrueCrimePhil
Twitter @TrueCrimePhil
YouTube @TrueCrimePhil

OUR WEBSITE

At PhilChalmers.com, you will be able to do the following:
Purchase resources from our website store, including autographed books.

Keep up with Phil Chalmers' tour dates so you can attend a live training. Download a media kit to assist you in bringing Phil and Wendi to your community for a live training or book signing appearance.

Email Phil and Wendi Chalmers, PhilChalmersTV@Gmail.com, or BookPhilChalmers@Gmail.com

Locate Phil Chalmers social media pages.

Download press photos.

PHIL CHALMERS' RESOURCES

In Phil Chalmers' website store, you can find the following merchandise and more:

The Teen Killer Whisperer Book, autographed. This is Phil's first 2019 release, and an update to the 2009 Inside the Mind of a Teen Killer. This book acts as a part two to Inside the Mind of a Teen Killer.

Inside the Mind of a Teen Killer book, autographed. This is Phil's major release and is the landmark book being used by law enforcement, colleges and the FBI pertaining to why teens kill, and how we stop them. This ten-year project is touted by many as the defining book about teen murder, including Lt Col Dave Grossman.

The Black Male Serial Killer, America's Newest Crime Wave, autographed. Phil Chalmers' first serial killer book, and will be released in 2020. This book tackles the many myths that people believe about today's serial killers, and this new groundbreaking research will surprise many, including those in law enforcement.

True Lies School Assembly Curriculum: For the first time ever, Phil Chalmers' powerful school assembly True Lies is now available as curriculum, and comes with Phil's slides, crime scene photos, script and the DVD. Phil wants as many people out there doing his assembly and helping him save as many kids as possible.

NEW! Stop Being a Little Bitch, autographed. This book will be released in 2020. This is Phil's motivational book for men.

YOU CAN BE A SPEAKER

Phil Chalmers has created the True Lies School Assembly Curriculum so you can perform it on your own. Phil has been speaking to students and teens for over thirty years, and he has decided it is time to share his information with others, so he can create an army of speakers all across the country. In this curriculum, you will get the following:

- DVD of Phil Chalmers performing the True Lies School Assembly
- PowerPoint slides that are the exact slides Phil uses in his school assembly
- Crime scene photos of a school shooting and an abduction to help you make a strong statement to the students
- A script of the exact words and approach Phil uses when he speaks
- A jump drive that includes the script, slides, photos and videos you will need for your assembly

TV SHOWS

Phil and Wendi Chalmers are currently developing a television show and documentary in which they will be interviewing serial killers, getting confessions, and solving cold cases. We will announce the date and location when it is ready for release, but it could land on a network like A&E or Netflix.

LIVE TRAINING

Phil and Wendi Chalmers speak at conferences, schools, colleges, police departments, and detention centers nationwide. You can track their tour schedule at PhilChalmers.com under Tour Dates, and if the event is public, you can attend. You can also bring Phil Chalmers to your city, conference or event. To do that, view Phil's tour schedule and choose an open date, and then email BookPhilChalmers@Gmail.com. Our office will send you the details, and let you know if Phil is available, and what his fee would be for the event you are requesting. Phil speaks to all types of adult groups, including police officers, teachers, school administrators, counselors, probation officers, first responders, military, department of corrections, legal teams, and to any adults who come into contact with juveniles. He can also be available for an evening community meeting for teachers, parents, administrators and students.

THANK YOU

We want to thank you for your support, love, and understanding about our passion to help stop teen violence and save innocent lives. We love our country, we love our God, and we love all people in this world. We hope that you steer clear of division, racism, sexism, homophobia, and hate, and love all people. We honor the military, our nation's flag, The President of the United States, our first responders, fire fighters, and all branches of law enforcement. We thank our military and law enforcement for keeping us safe, both in our great nation and abroad. Most of all, we love our God. We live by Phil's favorite verse, which he has tattooed on his chest: Philippians 4:13, "I can do all things through Christ who strengthens me."

God bless all of you, be safe, and keep up the great work. Keep fighting the good fight…it's valiant and noble to instill hope and value in our future generation, our most precious asset-our youth!

We hope to meet you on the road.

Phil and Wendi Chalmers
PhilChalmers.com
PhilChalmersTV@Gmail.com.

Printed in Great Britain
by Amazon

28563054R00090